6/13

WHAT WOULD JESUS DRINK?

== *A Spirit-Filled Study* ==

JOEL MCDURMON

TOLLE LEGE PRESS
WHITE HALL, WV

WHAT WOULD JESUS DRINK?

A Spirit-Filled Study

Copyright © 2011 by Joel McDurmon

Published by **Tolle Lege Press**
P.O. Box 5059
White Hall, WV 26555

Cover design by Joseph Darnell

Printed in the United States of America

Scripture quotations are taken from the Holy Bible: English Standard Version, copyright © 2001 by Crossway Bibles, a division of Good News Publishers, Wheaton, Illinois 60187.

ISBN 10: 0-9831457-4-1
ISBN 13: 978-0-9831457-4-5

To
the Vest family,
and
all the hospitable families of
Christ Church, Branch Cove

CONTENTS

"The sacred vine produced the prophetic cluster."

—St. Clement
Alexandria, 2nd Century

"We too often forbid maturity under the guise of purity."

—A Sage

FOREWORD
by Douglas Wilson

The Bible is a discomfiting book, for lots of people. It often says and teaches things we would rather not hear about, and represents God in ways that are disconcerting to those who would like to be known for their piety. But because man is devious, and has sought out many devices (Ecc. 7:29), we have developed various ways to work around this problem that the Bible creates. In theological circles, the ways of getting around what the Scriptures actually teach can be reduced to two broad categories—the liberal and the conservative approach.

The liberal approach rejects the practical authority of Scripture, but is oftentimes more to be trusted with what the text of Scripture actually says than the conservative approach is. This is true even though the conservatives are the ones who stoutly profess that the "Bible is the inerrant Word of God, without error in all that it affirms." The reason is because the liberal approach is not actually stuck with having to live with the results of the exegesis. Liberalism is the way of rejection, reserving the right to say that while the Bible may teach thus and such, "we have all grown past that now." This is why the liberal can acknowledge that the Bible teaches a particular doctrine, or sets before us a particular example, and then go on to say, "Wasn't that quaint? ho, ho, ho."

The conservative, on the other hand, has to live with what he claims the Bible says. If he doesn't want to live with it, if it conflicts with his traditions or most deeply cherished beliefs, then he has to make sure that his interpretation comes out in an acceptable fashion. Unlike the liberal, he does not have the option of acknowledging that Jesus drank wine, "but that He would have come to a more suitable position had His life not ended so tragically and so soon."

Thus it is ironic that many conservatives, who stand for the infallible authority of Scripture on every topic it addresses, are simply unwilling for the Bible to be okay with an amber bottle of Glenfiddich in a godly man's cabinet. But the Bible is okay with it (Dt. 14:26), and my chances of getting a liberal exegete to tell me what the text actually says on this point are better than getting a tee-totaling conservative to do so.

Ironically, many conservatives sheepishly acknowledge that the Bible does not prohibit the drinking of alcohol (quite the opposite), but go on to say that for the sake of a "good testimony" we should still swear off the stuff. Apart from the problems created by trying to have a better testimony than the Bible has, there is also the difficulty caused by the fact that tee-totalism provides its very own kind of bad testimony. H.L. Mencken was one of the leading infidel writers of the twentieth century, and he had no use for wowsers. They were, in short, a bad testimony. But in contrast, Mencken had this to say when a different kind of conservative, J. Gresham Machen, passed away.

When the Prohibition imbecility fell upon the country, and a multitude of theological quacks, including not a few eminent Presbyterians, sought to read support for it into the New Testament, he attacked them with great vigor, and routed them easily. He not only proved that there was nothing in the teachings of Jesus to support so monstrous a folly; he proved abundantly that the known teachings of Jesus were unalterably against it. And having set forth that proof, he refused, as a convinced and honest Christian, to have anything to do with the dry jehad.[1]

Machen had a good testimony (as biblically defined) because he was willing to say what the Bible said. He was willing to stick close to the text, which made him a true conservative. The Bible is not a blank screen onto which we may project our pious desires. The Bible is God's revealed Word to us, and as baptized Christians it is our responsibility to submit to it.

Like Machen, Joel McDurmon is my kind of conservative believer. He is willing to go where the Bible says we may go, even if that is the wine aisle of the supermarket. He is willing to sit down with the apostles to share a meal, even if the establishment serving lunch has beer on tap. He is willing to drink what the Bible says we may drink. And in this book, he does a fine job of setting before us the scriptural reasons for all of this. He begins where all our lessons in eating and drinking ought to begin, which is with the Lord's Supper, and he moves on to

---

1. From H.L. Mencken's obituary for J. Gresham Machen.

discuss the words the Holy Spirit chose to reveal His will on this subject. He then turns to address some common objections, which you have probably heard before. This is a small book, but there is a lot here.

I once read an odd throw-away line—I think it was the tag line on somebody's email—that has stuck with me in the years since first reading it. The statement goes right to the center of this issue, and illustrates why books like this small volume are so important. The line said, "If your pastor says that the wine in the Bible was grape juice, then how can you trust anything he says?"

This is a fine book, and I commend it to you.

Acknowledgments

I am indebted to two other learned books on this subject: Kenneth L. Gentry's *God Gave Wine: What the Bible Says About Alcohol*, and Jim West's *Drinking With Calvin and Luther: A History of Alcohol in the Church*. I have freely borrowed ideas from them (not always specifically attributed), and therefore most of the mistakes in this book are probably their fault. All the original thoughts and ideas herein, however, will hopefully keep me out of purgatory, especially since no such thing exists.

I also found inspiration over lunch with James B. Jordan, when he made comments about the theme of "Wine, Women, and Song" elaborated herein. I was not aware, until the later stages of writing this book, that he had already written and taught on it himself. I have not read or heard Jordan further on the theme, but I would expect the best in those efforts.

For other resources I have consulted, please see the "recommended reading" section in the back.

I also highly recommend that the truly blessed reader who wishes further insight on the subject pursue La Port du Ciel (2004). There is nothing better save the fullness of the Kingdom itself. All descriptions, theses, and dissertations of experts and theologians alike are bile in comparison.

Note to the Reader

If you are the type of person who can't wait, here's my answer: it is perfectly fine, right, Christian, biblical and godly to drink alcohol.

Not only is it incorrect, biblically speaking, to forbid others to drink beer, wine and/or strong liquor in general, it is downright sinful. One may even need to look into the possibility of whether forbidding enjoyment of alcohol is as sinful as the opposite extreme—drunkenness itself—if not more so. The drunkard forgets God; the prohibitionist *tries to be God.*

If, however, you are that patient type of person who likes to see the full maturation of the thought, the bouquet of reason and truth, then please accompany me for the following chapters. Taste and see that the Lord is *good.*

Part 1:
⇒ DiVine Glory ⇐

Chapter 1

A TALE OF TWO FEASTS

*"That you may learn to
fear the Lord your God always."*

The story of wine is a bit like the process of making wine: it starts off slow, requires patience and attention, and just as the fermentation process climaxes, you have to work, strain, fill casks, and then wait again. And finally, after long months and years of aging, a fine wine awaits in oak casks. Only then, after work and time—two of God's greatest gifts, next to wine—do we have the blessing of the finished product, a time truly to rest and relax, and the absolute bliss of that first kiss of wine on the tongue.

A taste of fine wine is a foretaste of the full bliss of the kingdom of God. The story begins with a hope and a promise, and finishes with a piece of the Promised Land. I invite you to begin that story here, with patience, and hope for a better understanding of God's finest way of life.

The Lamb and the Cup

One Spring morning when Jesus was twelve years old, he awoke to the bustle of his family preparing to travel. He knew where they planned to go; it was but a few days before the great feast of Passover, and his family every year devoutly made the pilgrimage to Jerusalem in order to keep the feast (according to Mosaic law, Deut. 16:1–8).

3

> Now his parents went to Jerusalem every year at the
> Feast of the Passover. And when he was twelve years
> old, they went up according to custom (Luke 2:41–42).

As they began the 65-mile journey due south, the
countryside of Nazareth stretched behind them: a val-
ley, where most homes in the village lay; fields of wild
flowers sloping upward to the base of high rising hills.
From one of these perches the boy would one day brush
with death at the hands of an angry mob (Luke 4). The
locals who had watched him grow up would simply not
believe that their own carpenter boy was the Messiah.
For now, the peaceful, agricultural landscape of small
rowed cornfields alongside olive and orange groves was
his home. For now, his family and the large group of locals shuffling down the dusty road to Jerusalem formed
his *community*.

Community was a defining feature of Jewish life and
theology (and in many places, still is). It was part of the
reason God gave them feasts to begin with. It would become even more important in the Great feast to come—
the one Jesus would commit to his followers.

On this particular occasion, the rabbis in Jerusalem
would learn this was no ordinary lad. And His mother's
twelve-year distant memories of the virgin birth of a holy
child, angelic messengers, and visits from distant magi
bearing gifts would get a strong jolt to recollection.

> And when the feast was ended, as they were return-
> ing, the boy Jesus stayed behind in Jerusalem. His
> parents did not know it, but supposing him to be in

the group they went a day's journey, but then they began to search for him among their relatives and acquaintances, and when they did not find him, they returned to Jerusalem, searching for him. After three days they found him in the temple, sitting among the teachers, listening to them and asking them questions. And all who heard him were amazed at his understanding and his answers. And when his parents saw him, they were astonished. And his mother said to him, "Son, why have you treated us so? Behold, your father and I have been searching for you in great distress." And he said to them, "Why were you looking for me? Did you not know that I must be in my Father's house?" And they did not understand the saying that he spoke to them. And he went down with them and came to Nazareth and was submissive to them. And his mother treasured up all these things in her heart (Luke 2:43–51).

The Passover was the feast commemorating God's deliverance of the Jews from Egypt. On that night, God had commanded the people to commemorate a time of haste; they were commanded to eat their Passover lamb with unleavened bread "with your belt fastened, your sandals on your feet, and your staff in your hand. And you shall eat it in haste" (Ex. 12:11). God was going to kill the first-born males of all the Egyptians that night, and the Jews were expected to be prepared to leave immediately. They were not allowed to eat leaven or to have leaven in their houses (Ex. 12:19–20), for the leavening process took time, and this was a time of haste.

Ironically (for a book on wine), there was no wine specified for the feast of the Passover. Much later, however, when Jesus would institute His own New Covenant meal at Passover, He would *specifically* include a cup of wine. We'll get to that in a minute.

In the story of the twelve-year-old Jesus at Passover, the young Lamb played out His own future sacrifice in a real-life drama, as it were. He leaves his parents (as if to cleave to a new bride, Gen. 2:24, the Church). They search for him among the travelling company, and with no success they return to Jerusalem in a panic. After three days they find him in the Temple. Here the Messiah is lost, disappears for three days, and then reappears in the temple—in other words, the Messiah dies, is buried three days, and then the true temple is resurrected.

Of course this is kind of deep; which is why even his own parents didn't understand what he was saying. After they chided Him because "your *father* [Joseph] and I have been searching," Jesus responds by reminding them who His true Father is, and thatHis business is His Father's business. He was conscious of the fact; but it may have been the first time Mary and Joseph (who knew His divine origins well) had been alerted to the fact that the young boy himself knew. Whatever the case, it was a Passover feast to remember. And we are told that Mary did, in fact, remember: "And his mother treasured up all these things in her heart."

Community

Notice, however, the vital aspect of community. Mary and Joseph did not even realize their son had gone missing until well into the journey home. How could such a parental oversight happen? Simple. Because parenting was in large part a community affair. (It's kind of like Hillary Clinton's "It Takes a Village," except there was no need for the thousands of federal government bureaucrats, noisy feminists, intrusive DHHS agents, arrogant and self-assured CPS social workers, nosy psychologists, CHIP or SCHIP, or Hillary Clinton—just the village). Jesus was not immediately by their side, but they assumed that He—as was normal—was with someone else in the group. So common was this practice that they rested assured on this assumption for a whole day (probably some 20 miles en route back home). When they thought of it, they began looking among all the people in the group. Where else would the boy be?

The community aspect of Jewish life—even in travelling long distances for observance of Holy days—was so taken for granted that a mother and father could assume *someone* they knew was watching their child without checking for the space of 24 hours.

This type of trusting fellowship and community was an important feature of Jewish life. Built right into their very religion, into the calendar they followed, was this series of feasts unto the Lord. They lived together, ate and drank together, celebrated together, traveled together . . . did everything together.

And this mentality continued right on into the early church (Acts 2:42). Except Jesus had made it even better: He introduced wine—not as an incidental "that's just what there is to drink" part of the meal, but as the key part of it. He made the wine the central focus of the Covenant.

Matthew, Mark, and Luke all record how Jesus used his last Passover to institute His New Covenant. He Himself fulfilled the true Passover—He himself was the sacrificial lamb, the meal:

> And when the hour came, he reclined at table, and the apostles with him. And he said to them, "I have earnestly desired to eat this Passover with you before I suffer. For I tell you I will not eat it until it is fulfilled in the kingdom of God." And he took a cup, and when he had given thanks he said, "Take this, and divide it among yourselves. For I tell you that from now on I will not drink of the fruit of the vine until the kingdom of God comes. And he took bread, and when he had given thanks, he broke it and gave it to them, saying, "This is my body, which is given for you. Do this in remembrance of me." And likewise the cup after they had eaten, saying, "This cup that is poured out for you is the new covenant in my blood" (Luke 22:14–20; see also Matt. 26:17–29; Mark 14:12–25).

We know the rest of the story: Jesus is betrayed, crucified, is buried, and then three days later rises from the grave.

So what does all of this have to do with wine and with community? There is a reason we call this New Testament meal "communion." There are several reasons, actually, but one that is important here. Paul explains it for us:

> The cup of blessing which we bless, is it not the communion of the blood of Christ? The bread which we break, is it not the communion of the body of Christ?

For we, though many, are one bread and one body; for we all partake of that one bread (1 Cor. 10:16–17, NKJV).

Paul shows here that in partaking of that special meal, we are displaying our oneness with Christ and with each other. We are one body (Christ's body), and we are blessed by one blood, Christ's blood.

As I said, Jesus took the wine and made it an integral part of the meal. In fact, He went so far as to say that the *cup "IS* the new covenant in my blood." He did not say this about the *bread*. The covenant is in the blood, in the cup.

While this may sound like some kind of theologian's hair to split, it has considerable significance. As we saw, the original Passover had not specified wine as an integral part. It featured bread. And in subsequent Old Testament rituals, bread also featured prominently—in fact, there was always bread in the temple, but not wine. Indeed, the Ark of the Covenant—on which was sprinkled the blood of the sacrifices—contained a pot of manna (a symbol of bread), but no wine.

In many cases, God commanded the priests to bring wine as a sacrifice along with an animal (we will talk about these a bit later), and while in each of these cases, the priests could consume the left-over sacrificed meat, they had to *pour out the wine.*

In fact, Old Testament priests, while on duty, were forbidden to drink wine:

And the Lord spoke to Aaron, saying, "Drink no wine or strong drink, you or your sons with you, when you go into the tent of meeting, lest you die. It shall be a statute forever throughout your generations" (Lev. 10:8–9).

So while wine and strong drink were not forbidden in society in general, the priests were forbidden to indulge while in the Holy Place. It is clear, then, that in the Old Testament, wine did not have a central role in the covenant between the people and God, and with each other.

But Jesus changed this. Why?

The New Covenant

Jesus gave us the meal as a New Covenant meal. And He specifically said the covenant was in the *cup*—not bread, or meat, or water, or anything else, but the cup which He held. It contained "the fruit of the vine"—that is, wine. This wine was "the new covenant in my blood." This is to say, the cup was a new version of the old Ark of the Covenant. Instead of the blood of animals being poured on it, it had the symbol of Christ's blood poured into it—wine. Wine was, therefore, the key symbol for the covenant, a key to understanding the kingdom.

As Passover was eaten in haste with no time for leavened bread, there certainly was no place for fermentation which takes even longer. Wine, therefore—which requires lengthy fermentation—is a symbol of stability, patience, endurance, perfection. These are the attributes of a long-term *Kingdom*, not people in transition or flux.

As a regular covenant meal, the wine of Communion reminds us of God's eternal kingdom. We have not yet arrived at its fullness, but we are given a foretaste of it in the glass of wine. As a covenant meal, we in effect renew that covenant with God and with each other every time we partake of that bread and wine. We renew our faith and affirmation in a long-term outlook of God's glorious kingdom.

When Jesus switched the emphasis of the Passover meal, he was saying, "Things have changed." From now on, the focus is not on the types and shadows of God's kingdom, but about the actual arrival of it. From now on, prepare to live life in God's kingdom.

For this reason, back in the types and shadows of God's kingdom in the Old Testament, we see recurring episodes of kings associated with wine. This was not in the capacity as civil decision-makers, mind you, for that God did not favor (Prov. 31:3–5); but in association with the whole idea of a prosperous, peaceful kingdom.

For example, when Abram defeated several gentile kings in Genesis 14, he ended by meeting with Melchizedek—"King of Righteousness," who was also a priest—and paid tithes to him. Melchizedek responded by offering Abram a covenant meal of bread and wine. When King David had fled due to the conspiracy of Absalom, a servant named Ziba met him on the Mount of Olives with loaves of bread and a bottle of wine (2 Sam. 16:1–5), expressing the faith of his master, "Today the house of Israel will give me back the kingdom of my father" (16:3). He was a little off on the timing, but David did regain the Kingdom, and Ziba an inheritance (2 Sam. 19:8ff; see v. 29). When Nehemiah grew sad in exile and prayed for his people to return and rebuild the walls of Jerusalem, the heathen king was sitting drinking wine (Neh. 2:1ff). In his lightened and more sensitive mood, the king gives Nehemiah authority to go. Throughout the book of Esther are featured banquets of wine thrown by the king. King Solomon brings his lover into his bedchambers with wine (Song 1:4). In each case, a new kingdom was coming into view, returning, or expanding in some way.

It was only fitting, then, that at the inauguration of His kingdom, Jesus would give His bride, His body, His people, wine. For wine is the symbol of Kingdom—the long-term, ever-maturing growth toward God's bliss.

Harvest

The Jews celebrated three harvest festivals each year: there were two grain harvests and a later fruit harvest. The earliest harvest coincided with the Passover, and marked the beginning of the grain harvest (Lev. 23:9–14). It was very important to the Jews to recognize God's providence in that earliest arrival of any produce. In the very onset they worshipped God for His providence by giving an offering from it. This took place in early spring every year.

Next came what was known as the feast of sevens, because it was held on the first day after seven weeks after Passover. Thus it was the "fifty days" festival, known by the Greek word for "fiftieth": "Pentecost." This was the rest of the grain harvest, and it also required an offering of "first fruits" (Lev. 23:15–21).

These two harvests only included grains—barley and wheat. Grapes would not be ready until the fall harvest. Thus by the time Pentecost rolled around each year, the only wine available could only have come from grapes pressed and bottled during the previous fall harvest—seven months earlier. Since there was no pasteurization or refrigeration back then, there is no possible way the wine at Passover and Pentecost could have been unfermented, alcoholic wine.[1] No wonder, then, that at the most famous feast of Pentecost when the disciples received the Spirit from God and spoke in other tongues, they were accused of being drunk on "sweet wine" (Acts 2:13, 15).

The theology is interesting here, too, insofar as the Hebrew festivals are fulfilled: the resurrected Christ is called the "first fruits" (1 Cor. 15:20, 23). He is the very first harvest from the dead. Meanwhile, the early Jews who were saved (before the Gospel reached the fullness including Gentiles as well, including 3,000 of the Jews from all over the world in Jerusalem at Pentecost, Acts 2:41) were called "first fruits" (James 1:18; Rev. 14:4). Until the Kingdom transition was fully completed with the destruction of the Jewish temple in AD 70, that early harvest of souls was only a "first fruit" (Rom. 8:23), a "down payment" or "earnest" (Eph. 1:14).

But then there was the grand finale of the harvest festivals—the "Feast of Booths" (or "tabernacles"). This took place at the end of the summer and celebrated the fullness of the fruit harvest being brought in (Lev. 23:33–43): olives, figs, dates, pomegranates, mulberries, and of course, grapes.

Since we have not yet reached the full harvest of souls for Jesus, we see no New Testament fulfillment of

---

1. See Garret Peck, "Winemaking in Ancient Israel," http://www.prohibitionhangover.com/israelwine.html (accessed February 14, 2011).

this passage. But this festival corresponds, theologically, to the fullness of God's Kingdom—a kingdom that began back at Pentecost.

"Learn to Fear the Lord your God Always"

Here's where the wine story gets really interesting. Old Testament law required a tithe to be paid on all the harvest, and all the tithe was to be brought to the central location God chose (Jerusalem). Of course, the occasion for this journey to Jerusalem would have coincided with the feast held precisely for that final harvest—the feast of booths. And when the Israelites got there, how were they to celebrate? Among other things, it was to be one big party. Here is how God Himself describes it in this law for tithing:

> You shall tithe all the yield of your seed that comes from the field year by year. And before the Lord your God, in the place that he will choose, to make his name dwell there, you shall eat the tithe of your grain, of your wine, and of your oil, and the firstborn of your herd and flock, that you may learn to fear the Lord your God always. And if the way is too long for you, so that you are not able to carry the tithe, . . . then you shall turn it into money and bind up the money in your hand and go to the place that the Lord your God chooses and spend the money for whatever you desire—oxen or sheep or wine or strong drink, whatever your appetite craves. And you shall eat there before the Lord your God and rejoice, you and your household (Deut. 14:22–26).

Notice several things about this great feast. First, God designed a feast in which His people eat the very meat, bread, and wine which they brought to tithe to Him. We should learn that organized feasting, paid for out of tithe money, is something of which God approves. Why? For three reasons which we have already been tracing: 1) Feasting builds community and communion among the covenant people; 2) It glorifies God in that the tithing and eating reminds us of His great and gracious providence for us; and 3) So that we, collectively as a covenant body of believers, "may learn to fear the Lord our God always."

Notice also that if the distance was too great to carry so many bundles upon bushels upon herds, etc., then you could sell your produce at a local market and bring the tithe in the form of money. Except, there was no offering plate: you were supposed to spend the money when you got to Jerusalem. And you were to spend it on meat, wine, strong drink, and whatever your appetite craved.

Now considering the grape harvest for this year would have just been harvested, it would have just been trampled and bottled as well. It may be tempting to think that the wine here would be the freshest, newest grape juice around. But as we shall see later, freshly-pressed wine was actually allowed to sit in open air and ferment for a few days before it was bottled. So even "new" wine was fermented. Besides, it is much more likely that they shelved the fresh for the following year and drank the last bottles of the previous vintage. It would have been the strongest stuff imbibed all year. This makes more sense of the text which couples the word "wine" with the word for "strong drink" which specifically refers to alcoholic drink.

In other words, God commanded His people to have a feast, and specified that it should include alcohol as far as their appetite craved it. This was to be God's way of celebrating the fullness of the harvest—the symbol of the fullness of the Kingdom.

The interesting thing about the great alcoholic celebratory feast of tabernacles is that we know Jesus attended it at least once. The story of Him going up to it appears in John 7. Did He join the feasting? What did His appetite crave? Did He drink wine and strong drink?

The text does not say, so it is equally possible that He did or did not. Considering that He went for the purpose of teaching (John 7:14, 37), it is possible He avoided drinking. But He is only said to have taught on two days. Since He had gone up in the middle of the seven-day feast (day four; see verse 14), He would have had two open days (five and six) in which to enjoy the party. It is hard to imagine He would not have engaged the feast in the way His Father had designed it originally. I tend to think He did enjoy Himself with food and drink in that way.

Even if He did not, it is pretty clear He understood the nature of the feast, and was expecting everyone else to be seeking to fulfill their appetites. For,

> On the last day of the feast, the great day, Jesus stood up and cried out, "If anyone thirsts, let him come to me and drink. Whoever believes in me, as the Scripture has said, 'Out of his heart will flow rivers of living water.'" Now this he said about the Spirit, whom

those who believed in him were to receive, for as yet the Spirit had not been given, because Jesus was not yet glorified (John 7:37–39).

Jesus' teaching here was not out of the blue. He knew people had filled Jerusalem to consume whatever their hearts desired. He challenged them to thirst for something eternal. He was not denying the enjoyment they found in the meat and strong drink. He was rather using that enjoyment as a foretaste of something greater which He announced. For that purpose, the abundance of harvest, the savor of roasted meat, the bliss of wine—were all vitally important as part of His religion and society in general. It was just now time to see the fullfillment of what those pleasures foreshadowed: the Messiah Himself.

Conclusion

Now, how often has your pastor preached that your church should 1) have a yearly feast, 2) allowing for wine and strong drink, and 3) paid for with your tithe money? How distant is it from the mind of the average Christian preacher today that we should even imbibe alcohol, let alone pay for it with our tithes?

I personally think churches should refocus on organized rejoicing in this manner. Bring out the wine, beer, scotch, and whatever else we want, and declare a feast unto the Lord. Schedule it and publish to all the congregation. It would make the church more biblical, and it may even bring in some of the lost sheep who stay away because church so often seems cold, strict, abstract, and opposed to enjoyment. We should be an example to the world that "whatever your appetite craves" is not necessarily forbidden, but should be used with maturity and dominion.

It would also 1) foster a stronger sense of community among the body of believers, 2) charge them with a sense of the great blessings we have in God's abundant providence for us, and 3) remind us that in everything—even in enjoyment—we can and should fear God.

This "Tale of Two Feasts" is about the Bible's inclusion of wine in Passover and in the feast of booths. It is about the new covenant in Jesus' cup, and Jesus' bringing in of the fullness of the Kingdom of God. As we saw Jesus earlier making the wine a central focus of Passover, and God teaching us to celebrate His providence with alcohol, we should learn to enjoy wine and strong drink as foretastes of the great Kingdom bliss to come.

Chapter 2

AND NOAH PLANTED
A VINEYARD

Imagine yourself standing on top of the world, and you could do just about anything you wanted. Except there was one catch: no one else existed except you and your immediate family. What would you do?

That's pretty much where Noah found himself after the flood waters receded. He was standing atop the mountains of Ararat, and he had the whole rest of his life ahead of him.

But it was kind of lonely. He had only his wife, his three sons, and their three wives as company. What was he going to do? It's not like there was much of a job market. All the local businesses had, well, gone under. Noah had shipbuilding skills, but the shipyards were sunk, the Shipbuilders Union bust, and Noah didn't like unions anyway. So he scratched his head.

Then he remembered the promise God made to him. On the day he exited the ark, on the same day he made an altar and a sacrifice to God, the Lord said, "I will never again curse the ground because of man. . . . While the earth remains, seedtime and harvest, cold and heat, summer and winter, day and night, shall not cease" (Gen. 8:21–22).

"Never again curse the ground." "Seedtime and harvest." The promises seemed to have a theme.

Noah decided to become a farmer. And in becoming a farmer, Noah decided to plant grapes:

Noah began to be a man of the soil, and he planted a vineyard. He drank of the wine and became drunk and lay uncovered in his tent (Gen. 9:20–21).

This is the first mention of wine in the Bible. (Consequently, when looking for a "beginning" of something in the Bible, Genesis is a good place to start. "Genesis" means "beginning," literally.)

In these primary verses of our subject, we find three important terms for our study: 1) vineyard, 2) wine, and 3) drunk. Of course, the key word here is the last of the three: drunk. This pretty well establishes everything we need to know about the "wine" in this verse—it is certainly fermented wine, alcoholic enough to lead to drunkenness. It was not mere grape juice. (We'll talk about "drunk" more in a minute.)

There's some good theology here, too. In planting a vineyard, Noah had become a "man of the soil." "Soil" translates the Hebrew word *adamah*, which is the standard word for dirt or soil. But note the word *Adam* within that word *adamah*. This is no accident. There's always been a correlation between man (Adam) and the soil from which he was taken. This is explicit in Hebrew theology. God formed *Adam* from the *adamah*, the dust of the earth (Gen 2:7). We know that we shall return to that dust due to God's judgment on sin and death. Noah, however, was saved from judgment by God's grace, endured the flood, and stood on the other side of it. In a very real sense he represented Adam baptized in the flood and resurrected—a new *man of the soil*. The new Adam, of course, would be fully realized in the person of the resurrected Jesus Christ.

Peter uses this exact teaching:

> God's patience waited in the days of Noah, while the ark was being prepared, in which a few, that is, eight persons, were brought safely through water. Baptism, which corresponds to this, now saves you, not as a removal of dirt from the body but as an appeal to God for a good conscience, through the resurrection of Jesus Christ (1 Pet. 3:20–22).

Noah certainly stood as a figure of the saved and baptized believer resurrected as a new man in Christ. We are new Adams—new men of the soil, so to speak—just as Noah.

It is interesting, perhaps only as a coincidence, that when real wine connoisseurs taste wine, the key taste they *don't* want to taste is grape juice. Instead, they want to taste *the soil*.

While tasting soil may sound strange to many novice wine drinkers, the industry considers it fundamental. Especially to Old World winemakers, something called *terroir*—a word that ultimately means "land"—has profound influence on the wine. The local qualities of soil, climate, environment, etc., make each wine unique when developed properly. Again, these features point back to local community, as well as our earthly origin.

Noah's Wine

We noted in the episode of Noah's vineyard that "wine" in that verse is alcoholic. The important thing about this first mention of wine in the Bible is that the Hebrew word used for "wine" is a standard word used throughout the Hebrew text for that purpose: the word *yayin*. It is used 140 times in the Old Testament. The Hebrew language uses a few other words to mean "wine" also, and we will look at those momentarily. For now, let us consider a little more about *yayin*.

Hebrew scholars say that *yayin* comes from an "unused root," which means that despite flipping through lots of books and ancient records, Hebrew scholars have not found any texts using the most basic form of the word. At this point, they usually take a break and have a beer. They do know, however, that the root word actually *means* "to effervesce"—that is, to create lots of bubbles. This pretty clearly references the fermentation process where yeast converts sugars into ethyl alcohol and carbon dioxide. While this process occurs in a vat of mashed grapes and their juice, over time, teams of tiny bubbles escape (the carbon dioxide). Thus it seems obvious that the very Hebrew word for wine is descriptive of grape juice that has undergone this bubbly process.

So from the very meaning of the word itself, and from Noah's drunkenness in the very first usage of that word in the Bible, we can see that biblical wine is alcoholic wine.

Scripture uses the word in a context that demands intoxicating wine so many other times that it's impossible to deny. Here's what happens when people drink too much *yayin*:

- Noah gets drunk on it (Gen. 9:20–21).
- Lot gets drunk on it (Gen. 19:32–35).
- Ahasuerus was "merry" with it (Esther 1:10–11).
- It makes people stagger (Ps. 60:3).
- The proverbial drunkard has all kinds of personal issues because of it (Prov. 23:29–35).
- The "drunkards of Ephraim" were overcome by it (Is. 28:1).
- The Babylonian empire is drunk on it (Hab. 2:5).

If that ain't intoxicating stuff, I don't know what is.

Meanwhile, drunkenness is often mentioned in general reference to feasting. While *yayin* is not always mentioned, it is assumed that it was the standard drink for the occasion. In other words, whatever the standard drink was at the time, it was assumed to have been able to intoxicate. See the instances with Nabal (1 Sam. 25:36–37), Uriah (2 Sam. 11:13), Elah (1 Kings 16:9), and Ben-Hadad (1 Kings 20:16). In short, wine in the Bible is alcohol unless explicitly specified otherwise.

Disputes

This understanding is important today because some Christians are either unaware of the facts or unwilling to face them. But trying to hide such a flood of facts with one's own prejudice is kind of like trying to contain a keg in a teacup.

Nevertheless, many Christian preachers and scholars have written books wishing to impose their anti-alcohol agenda on Scripture—trying to replace the plain and common sense language of the text with dry-friendly interpretations.

Take Stephen M. Reynolds for example. He's a scholar trained in ancient Semitic languages who helped translate the New International Version of the Bible. Of all people you would think he would look at the word itself and its usages in Scripture and conclude that *yayin* has intoxicating properties.

But Dr. Reynolds is a Christian who first believes that Christians should never imbibe alcohol in any quantities or under any conditions. It appears that his strong belief leads him to look for evasions of the plain meaning. He complains about the consistent translation of *yayin* as "wine": "There is a word *must* which could be used.... This by definition would be a good word to substitute for wine when the sense of Scripture demands it."[1]

But there is at least one verse containing *yayin* that really paints the prohibitionist scholar into a corner. Isaiah 25:6 is a prophecy of good times to come: "On this mountain the Lord of hosts will make for all peoples a feast of rich food, a feast of well-aged wine, of rich food full of marrow, of aged wine well refined." The phrase "well-aged wine" comes from the Hebrew word *shemarim*, which refers to the sediment or dregs left at the bottom of a wine vat after the wine has fermented. This is a particular reference to carefully aged, fully matured wine, and thus obviously fully fermented. In

---

1. Quoted in Gentry, 36–37.

other words, when God decides to bring a great blessing to His people, He provides a great feast with wine that we know is alcoholic.

Even more interesting than this, the rest of the passage reveals that this is no random feast. This feast is *messianic*. It is a celebration of God's salvation of His people and triumph over death itself:

> And he will swallow up on this mountain the covering that is cast over all peoples, the veil that is spread over all nations. He will swallow up death forever; and the Lord God will wipe away tears from all faces, and the reproach of his people he will take away from all the earth, for the Lord has spoken. It will be said on that day, "Behold, this is our God; we have waited for him, that he might save us. This is the Lord; we have waited for him; let us be glad and rejoice in his salvation" (Is. 25:7–9).

It's no wonder that the Christian feast Christ gave us as a memorial of His death is a feast of bread and wine.

Yet our prohibitionist brethren cannot even accept this clear passage. Despite having absolutely no viable way of refuting it, they refuse to accept it. Reynolds, for example, says, "The improbable must be the correct answer. . . . It is true that the lexicographers do not recognize any other meaning for *shemer* than dregs, lees or sediment, but we must face the improbable answer that they are incorrect in this particular verse."[2] The prohibitionist, in other words, values his personal bias at the

---

2. Quoted in Gentry, 36.

expense of plain truth.

Thankfully, not all Christian scholars who person-ally oppose the use of alcohol also oppose the clear meaning of the text. One such scholar, R. Laird Har-ris, who is an author and editor of the widely-used and accepted *Theological Wordbook of the Old Testament*, concludes of the word *yayin*: "its intoxicating proper-ties are mentioned at least twenty times," and it "was the most intoxicating drink known in ancient times."[3] In fact, *yayin* is so obviously intoxicating that Harris notes it is "frequently condemned, often associated with drunkenness, and seldom spoken of in any favor-able light."[4] Another similar and well-known scholar, Merrill Unger, says basically the same thing: "[I]n most of the passages in the Bible where *yayin* is used ... it certainly means fermented grape juice, and in the re-mainder it may be fairly presumed to do so. In no case can it be positively shown to have any other meaning. The intoxicating character of *yayin* in general is plain from Scripture."[5]

Of course, we could just as easily arrive at this posi-tion from the simple lesson of Noah. He planted a vine-yard, drank the *yayin*, and got drunk. No doctorate in Semitic languages is needed here.

Drinking "Drunkenness" Itself

As we have seen, Noah planted a vineyard, drank wine and it made him drunk. We talked briefly about the vine-

---

3. Quoted in Gentry, 34.
4. Quoted in Gentry, 38–39.
5. Quoted in Gentry, 38.

yard, and more particularly about the soil. We have done a little biblical word study of the word for wine, *yayin*. This was the second of the three main points in that story from Genesis 9:20–21. Let us now look at what I said was the key to understanding the wine in this passage: the word "drunk."

We have already seen one reason why "drunk" is a key here: it directly demonstrates that the wine spoken of here was fermented wine, not grape juice. And since this is the most common word for wine throughout the Old Testament, it's a pretty good indicator that in the Old Testament, wine in general is an intoxicating beverage. There are a few minor exceptions to this, but we will look at them later.

An even more startling reason why this word for "became drunk" is important is that Hebrew sometimes uses the word to refer to the fermented drink itself. For starters, in the Noah passage the word for "drunk" is *shakar*. The word is actually a verb: "get drunk" or "become drunk." In other places it is used in a noun form, *shekar*—"drunkenness" or "intoxication."

In just one example, when the priest Eli finds Hannah praying quietly near the tabernacle, he sees her lips moving but hears no words. He accuses her of being drunk: "How long will you go on being drunk [*shakar*]? Put your wine away from you" (1 Sam. 1:14). But he had misjudged the situation. Hannah responded, "No, my lord, I am a woman troubled in spirit. I have drunk neither wine [*yayin*] nor strong drink [*shekar*], but I have been pouring out my soul before the Lord" (1 Sam. 1:15). Notice here how both words are linked with the effect: *yayin* and *shekar* can make a person *shakar,* become drunk.

Shekar is often translated "strong drink." Considering the strict relation between the verb form and the noun, we might accurately call the drink itself "intoxication." When one imbibes it, they could be said literally to be drinking intoxication itself.

We should be careful, of course, not to go too far with this thought. It does not mean that by merely drinking wine or liquor one is in fact getting drunk to the point of excess—the modern sense of the word. It simply refers to the natural influence of alcohol which is not yet to the point of excess and loss of control. And since a phrase like "drinking drunkenness" is so clumsy, I doubt anyone would ever use it anyway. I include it here only to show how directly Scripture connects the drink itself with the potential effects of the drink. This connection is made at the very level of the word itself.

It is best to understand Scripture as saying that we can enjoy alcohol for its enjoyable nature and effects. We should not abuse it, of course; that goes without saying. But we absolutely are allowed—and should—enjoy it for what it is and does for us.

Whatever Your Appetite Craves

While many of the biblical uses of *shekar* report or warn against instances of abuse, this is not universally so. In fact, some very important instances show quite the opposite. In the very passage we examined in the last chapter—the yearly tithe festival (Deut. 14:22–26)— God specifically commands His people to use a tithe of their income toward a massive feast. And in this feast,

God commands that we should *enjoy ourselves* through food and drink, specifically allowing wine (*yayin*), strong drink (*shekar*), and "whatever your appetite craves" (Deut. 14:26).

Strong Drink for Jesus

Scripture uses strong drink positively in other places as well. For example, God required food offerings for Himself. Among these, a drink offering was required, and it had to be strong drink by God's command: "Its drink offering shall be a quarter of a hin for each lamb. In the Holy Place you shall pour out a drink offering of strong drink [*shekar*] to the Lord" (Num. 28:7).

A hin is about a gallon. So a quarter of a hin is roughly a quart. This was to be offered twice daily—morning and evening (Num. 28:1–8). God's personal food requirement was a whole lamb and a quart of strong drink at breakfast and for dinner. He requested it both as "food" and as "a pleasing aroma." These things we can relate to. God is a God of Providence and Pleasure. The important thing to note here is that when He could have required simply water or any other available drink, He commanded the strongest thing available—strong drink (*shekar*)—for Himself. If it's good enough for Him. . . .

The Twelve Tribes of Shekar

Finally, for now (although this certainly does not exhaust all the uses of the word in the Bible), look at the feast that Joseph threw for his brothers in Egypt. While they had not yet recognized who he was, Joseph threw a feast and lined them up at the table according to their birthright—oldest to youngest. The Bible says, "Portions were taken to them from Joseph's table, but Benjamin's portion was five times as much as any of theirs. And they drank and were merry with him" (Gen. 43:34).

The Hebrew text, however, says something more revealing than the English translators were willing to admit: it says "they drank and *shakar* with him."[6] That is, they drank with him until they were all clearly under the influence. They *enjoyed themselves*.

Unfortunately, most of our modern English translations tend to paper-mache over the clear meaning. They say things like "were merry" (KJV, ESV, NRS) or "drank freely" (NAS, NIV, NJB, NLT, TM). These translations all do this, I think, in order to avoid saying that Joseph and his brothers all got drunk; but this is unnecessary. It is not difficult to translate the passage more accurately and honestly without condemning the Patriarchs as drunkards. "They drank and became relaxed with him." At least one of the paraphrase translations gets close: "So Joseph's brothers drank with him and had a good time" (CEV).

The great Reformer, John Calvin, notices the word in his classic commentary on Genesis. His comments are worth reading:

> For the word שכר (*shakar*,) they "were merry," signifies, either that they were not always accustomed to drink wine, or that there was more than ordinary indulgence at the sumptuous tables

---

6. For you scholars out there, I recognize that actual text has the verb in the Qal Imperfect, third person plural—*yishkru*. I use the root form in the text above for the ease of the average reader.

spread for them. Here, however, no intemperance
is implied, (so that drunkards may not plead the
example of the holy fathers as a pretext for their
crime,) but *an honorable and moderate liberality.*
I acknowledge, indeed, that the word has a dou-
ble meaning, and is often taken in an ill sense;
as in Genesis 9:21, and in similar places: but in
the present instance the design of Moses is clear.
Should any one object, that a frugal use of food
and drink is simply that which suffices for the
nourishing of the body: I answer, although food is
properly for the supply of our necessities, yet the
legitimate use of it may proceed further. For it is
not in vain, that our food has savor as well as vital
nutriment; but thus our heavenly Father sweetly
delights us with his delicacies. And his benignity
is not in vain commended in Psalm 104:15, where
he is said to create "wine that maketh glad the
heart of man."[7]

As I said, God is a God of both Providence and Pleasure. The counterpart to that is that we—His image—are
a people of both duty and delight. I appreciate Calvin's
phrase "moderate liberality." I think it should be the
model of how we approach alcohol—with wise Christian
judgment and self-control in the midst of freedom and
enjoyment. I think that moderate liberality should be
the model of how we do everything in the Christian life.

---

7.   John Calvin, *Commentaries on the First Book of Moses
Called Genesis*, trans. by John King (Grand Rapids, MI: Eerdmans,
1948), 362–3. I have updated the style of his Scripture references.

Instead of "Do not handle, Do not taste, Do not touch" (Col. 2:21) which Paul condemns, we should learn how to handle abundance and freedom.

Paul elsewhere said, "I know how to be brought low, and I know how to abound" (Phil. 4:12). Christians in our culture have had plenty of being brought low, but we have done very poorly at learning how to abound.

Chapter 3

WHAT *DID* JESUS DRINK?

The best way to learn exactly what Jesus *would* drink is to do a study of the Gospels to find out exactly what He *did* drink. This seems like common sense. Of course, it will also help to have some understanding of the social and historical background of Jesus' times. We've already learned some of this in the first chapter. This helps us know the extent of what kinds of drinks would have been available, what was common, and what the Bible most likely means when it speaks of certain kinds of drinks. So, in this chapter we will investigate the biblical and historical data of what Jesus actually *did* drink.

To find out what kinds of things Jesus actually did drink, it makes sense just to read the Gospels and find out. What do they say that Jesus actually drank?

Surprising Silence

The answer will surprise many Christians. In fact, it surprised this author quite a bit. The Gospels nowhere say that Jesus drank wine! Go ahead, do a search for yourself: the Gospels nowhere explicitly say that Jesus drank wine.

But the surprise, however, is really more than this. The Gospels never explicitly record Jesus drinking *anything*. Nothing. Not even water. (There is one tiny exception here, which I will discuss in a moment.)

This is shocking because so many people answer the wine question too quickly: "Well, Jesus drank wine."

They have in mind, probably, the wedding at Cana where Jesus turned water into wine, or the Last Supper where Jesus gave the bread and wine to His apostles. But this is not quite accurate. In neither of these instances are we told that Jesus Himself actually drank the wine. In fact, the accounts of the Supper seem to indicate that He did not drink the wine:

> And he took a cup, and when he had given thanks he said, "Take this, and divide it among yourselves. For I tell you that from now on I will not drink of the fruit of the vine until the kingdom of God comes" (Luke 22:17–18; see also Matt. 26:26–28; Mark 14:22–24).

It is unclear whether this means He would not drink it again after drinking this one last time, or whether His voluntary abstinence included this meal.

Now this silence may seem to place a stumbling block in the path of the theory that Jesus in fact *did* drink wine or any kind of alcohol. Since Scripture never explicitly says He did, then we have no explicit proof that He did. But to argue this way would commit a classic fallacy—an argument from silence. Such reasoning—were we to follow it to its logical conclusion—would lead to an absurdity. In its silence on the subject of Christ's drinking, the Bible includes not just wine but *all* drinks, even water. Were we to follow the reasoning that "silence" means "abstinence," we must also argue that Jesus abstained from all juices as well as water His whole life. While we know that He did fast in this manner once for forty days prior to His temptation in the wilderness (Matt. 4), to

argue that He maintained a completely drinkless diet
for His full 33 years would be the height of absurdity. In
fact, since the Bible never explicitly says Jesus nursed at
His mother's breast, we must—to be consistent with this
logic—assume that He abstained from that drink as well.

The only exception to the silence is in John 19:28–30.
When Jesus was crucified, right before His death, soldiers gave Him vinegar on a sponge. While the accounts
all have Jesus rejecting the soldiers' first attempt, John
records that He "received" the second one:

> After this, Jesus, knowing that all was now finished,
> said (to fulfill the Scripture), "I thirst." A jar full of
> sour wine stood there, so they put a sponge full of
> the sour wine on a hyssop branch and held it to his
> mouth. When Jesus had received the sour wine, he
> said, "It is finished," and he bowed his head and gave
> up his spirit.

The "sour wine" here is essentially vinegar—wine
that has been exposed to oxygen too long and has soured.
Soldiers were allowed to keep it in rations in case they
were wounded mortally in battle; it helped ease the pain.
They apparently kept it on hand for victims of crucifix-
ions as well.

We are specifically told that Jesus received some of it,
and that He did so in order to fulfill the Scriptures—in
other words, to fulfill prophecy. There are two particular
prophecies involved here, both from the Psalms. Some
think that Psalm 22—a classic prophecy of the crucifix-
ion of the Messiah—is in view here:

My strength is dried up like a potsherd,
and my tongue sticks to my jaws;
you lay me in the dust of death (Ps. 22:15).

While this is possibly the reference to Jesus thirsting, I think the whole episode is captured more in a different place:

Reproaches have broken my heart,
so that I am in despair.
I looked for pity, but there was none,
and for comforters, but I found none.
They gave me poison for food,
and for my thirst they gave me sour wine to drink
(Ps. 69:20–21).

While Jesus was clearly not drinking for pleasure here, it is interesting that in this only explicit reference to Jesus drinking anything in Scripture, that drink is alcoholic. And in this instance, it was mandatory that He drink it, so that prophecy could be fulfilled.

Whether Jesus Himself drank wine or not, it is clear that He approved of drinking alcohol, for as we have seen, the wine at Passover had to have been alcoholic; and now we learn that at the Last Supper He *commanded* His disciples all to drink it.

Vines Between the Lines

I have only dealt so far with *explicit* references to what Jesus drank, but I make this point for a reason. It is important to understand that sometimes the best (or even only) way to interpret Scripture is to read between the lines, so to speak—to draw implications, logical inferences and deductions, and to examine poetry and imagery and how the prophets and Jesus used them. All of these things are quite profitable to the Bible student, especially in the absence of any explicit references we would otherwise hope to see.

The Gospels are helpful in this way. A good instance regards how Jesus' opponents condemned Him and John the Baptist:

> John the Baptist has come eating no bread and drinking no wine, and you say, "He has a demon." The Son of Man has come eating and drinking, and you say, "Look at him! A glutton and a drunkard, a friend of tax collectors and sinners!" Yet wisdom is justified by all her children (Luke 7:33–35; see also Matt. 11:18–19).

This shows how Jesus' enemies could never be persuaded—not because of a lack of truth, but because they refused to be persuaded by anything. They would always find some reason to reject the truth, even if it contradicted the reason they rejected it last time. In this case, they condemned John the Baptist for not drinking wine, and then condemned Jesus for drinking wine!

Now this pretty much implies that Jesus did, in fact, drink wine, regularly. However, we have to remember that this was an accusation of Jesus' opponents, so they may have been lying about Him (they do bring up false witnesses against Him later, in fact: see Matt. 26:59–60). But this is Jesus telling His version of the argument: it seems that if this were a false accusation, Jesus would have said so. We know that the first part of the argument—concerning John the Baptist—is factual. He seems to have been set apart by the special voluntary vow of the "Nazirite" (see Numbers 6) in which the individual taking the vow abstained from all fruit of the vine, including wine, juice, raisins, etc. Everything. This is said of John the Baptist: "he will be great before the Lord. And he must not drink wine or strong drink, and he will be filled with the Holy Spirit, even from his mother's womb" (Luke 1:15).

There is, therefore, no reason to doubt the truth of the second part of Jesus' statement: that He Himself in fact did eat and drink. It was well known that Jesus *did* eat openly with publicans and sinners (Luke 5:29–35), and Jesus defended Himself doing so. And since the reference to John the Baptist drinking was to wine, and since Jesus was accused of being a glutton and a *drunkard*, it stands to reason that Jesus in fact drank alcoholic wine. Of course, we assume that He never drank to excess: this accusation was merely convenient for His enemies and had no basis in fact.

What this shows, moreover, is how some people refuse to acknowledge the truth right in front of their eyes. Instead, they rationalize the situation so as to favor their own already-decided biases. Confronted with the truth of John the Baptist, the Pharisees refused to repent. They called him demon possessed based on his constant fasting, praying, and seclusion. But faced with someone who had the same message, and yet did not do those things, they still refused to repent, and accused Him of excess in eating and drinking.

This is called cognitive dissonance. The Pharisees were the puritans in town, and they led most Jewish social efforts at education and lay-ministry in studying the law. They were the respected teachers of the people. When John and Jesus began drawing large crowds, these established leaders became jealous. Instead of repenting and embracing the Messiah as they should have, they began to make every excuse in the book to justify their own position: John had a demon, Jesus was a drunk, no prophet could come from Galilee (John 7:52), and many other false witnesses. Instead of changing their own beliefs, they rationalized. They had even witnessed Jesus' miracles. One thing was sure: whatever confronted them, no matter how divine, they would not be persuaded. They would hold to their twisted perversion of God's truth to the bitter end.

This is very similar, by the way, to how many Christians today defend total abstinence from alcohol. Although the Bible features the enjoyment of alcohol in many places, they adamantly hold their own Pharisaical prohibitions. Based on this up-front prejudice, they will ignore, dismiss, or reinterpret every passage in the Bible that speaks positively of wine. They will preach hard on the negative passages. They will apply the negative passages against drunkenness to *all* consumption of alcohol, and they will make unwarranted divisions in the meaning of the words. Their dissonance is sometimes transparent: for example, they often say that "wine" (*yayin* in Hebrew, or *oinos* in Greek) means "grape juice," not fermented, unless it is in connection with drunkenness, in which case it is already condemned. As we have seen so far, this is impossible and ridiculous. I will deal more with these types in a later chapter. For now, it is enough to see the type of rationalizing that goes on in the Pharisaical mindset, and how that mindset is still with us today.

Jesus' Culture

In Jesus' time, wine was the most widely used and safest beverage. We have already discussed the yearly feasts timed according to the agricultural cycles. We saw how only alcoholic wine would have been available at Passover, and how even the freshest bottled juice would still already have been fermented. Remember also that in those times and in that place, water was a scarce resource. A well was a prized treasure, and was held dear for centuries. The woman at the well in John 4 was drawing from Jacob's well (John 4:12); it had thus been around for roughly 1800 years at that time.

Wine on the other hand was plentiful. The yearly grape harvest was immediately treaded out in presses that were chiseled out of pure limestone. The juice ran into large chiseled-out pits and was left in the open air to begin fermenting. We mentioned tasting the soil earlier. The modern day investigator notes this feature of open-air fermentation: "Fermentation was done in the open air for up to a week, during which dust and dirt could mix in with the wine, giving new meaning to terroir."[1] After a few days, the wine was bottled in new goatskins (*new skins*, to allow for stretching due to further fermenta-

---

1.   Garret Peck, "Winemaking in Ancient Israel," http://www.prohibitionhangover.com/israelwine.html (accessed February 14, 2011).

tion), making the feast of tabernacles a glorious celebration for people, and a bad day for goats.

The trampling/pressing process was so widespread that within the area of only a single modern-day winery in Israel, archaeologists have unearthed over a hundred of these ancient winepresses.[2] There must, then, have been tens of thousands, maybe hundreds of thousands, across the whole land of Israel. In Jesus' days, these all would have been producing wine every year.

The wine was also safer to drink than water. Water that was drawn and stored was easily corrupted by bacteria, etc., and could lead to sickness and disease. For this reason we see Paul instructing Timothy to stop drinking it: "No longer drink only water, but use a little wine for the sake of your stomach and your frequent ailments" (1 Tim. 5:23).

This is not, as many people seem to think, saying that we should use wine for medicinal purposes only. This was instructing Timothy to stop drinking the water and start drinking wine regularly because of his stomach problems (obviously caused by drinking the water). In fact, the word "only" does not even appear in the original text (why the ESV translators added it is not clear). It should read "No longer drink water," or "Drink no more water." Ironically, far from a biblical prohibition against wine, here we have a biblical prohibition against water! (At least, in a qualified sense.)

---

2. Garret Peck, "Winemaking in Ancient Israel," http://www.prohibitionhangover.com/israelwine.html (accessed February 14, 2011).

Note also that without wine, Timothy was getting sick *frequently*. Wine was not something to be kept around for the once-in-a-while event of an illness; it was to be used regularly as a preventative measure. Paul was enjoining the regular drinking of wine because without it, Timothy was *frequently* getting sick because of the water.

So, wine was more sanitary than the water; and it was also in greater supply. This situation was so firmly the case in the ancient Middle East that it sometimes remains so today in Israel. One modern day writer on alcohol relates a relevant anecdote that says it all:

> When I attended the Israwinexpo 2008, a biannual event in Tel Aviv to draw international attention to Israeli wine, I learned just how scarce water can be in Israel. A winemaker rinsed my wineglass with wine instead of water, swirled it around, then dumped it out. He joked, "In Israel, we have more wine than water" as he refilled it with another wine sample to taste.[3]

Conclusion

This brief study of "What *Did* Jesus Drink?" has taught us a couple of things. First, we learned that it is wrong to argue from silence. Jesus is not specifically said to have drunk anything except a sip of vinegar on the cross. If this silence means Jesus never drank wine, it also means He never drank anything else. This is absurd.

---

3.   Garret Peck, "Winemaking in Ancient Israel," http://www.prohibitionhangover.com/israelwine.html (accessed February 14, 2011).

Secondly, we learned that sometimes we need to read between the lines. In Jesus' culture, alcoholic wine was so integral to life that it is unthinkable that Jesus never drank it—either at celebratory feasts, or as part of everyday life. In fact, wine was much safer to drink than water, as it is in many places still today. And the gospel incidents make it clear that Jesus ate and drank with publicans and sinners, that these people normally drank wine (and sometimes were known for getting drunk), and that Jesus himself was accused of drunkenness because he ate and drank with them. He surely must have been drinking the same wine as they, although not to excess as they may have.

In short, it is inconceivable that Jesus never drank wine. But even on the remote chance that He did not, we know that on at least two occasions, He purposefully gave it to other people to drink: at the wedding at Cana, and to His disciples at the Last Supper. Apparently, He well approved of them drinking alcohol. And personally, I'm quite sure He drank it, and enjoyed it, too.

Chapter 4

WINE, WOMEN, AND SONG

The Bible advocates wine as a celebratory blessing, and as a healthful regular beverage. Wine symbolizes pleasure and a foretaste of the fullness of the Kingdom to come. Pleasure and bliss are, therefore, very important aspects of God's growing kingdom now.

This is why the Psalmist speaks of wine as making the heart glad:

> You cause the grass to grow for the livestock
> and plants for man to cultivate,
> that he may bring forth food from the earth
> and wine to gladden the heart of man,
> oil to make his face shine
> and bread to strengthen man's heart (Ps. 104:14–15).

While there are many passages dealing with wine and alcohol throughout Scripture, it is here more than any other place that we get a clear statement on the *purpose* of wine: it is to gladden the heart of man.

This should be read in the context of all of Psalm 104: it is about God's glory as the Creator, the splendor of His creation, and His gracious providence in that created order.

> O Lord, how manifold are your works!
> In wisdom have you made them all;
> the earth is full of your creatures (104:24).

Part of this order involves His provision for His creatures: "living things both small and great," even "Leviathan, which you formed to play in it. These all look to you, to give them their food in due season" (104:25–27). Notice that man, however, the image of God Himself, is given more than just nourishment: he is given *enjoyment* and *beauty*. Not only does man have "food," but "wine to gladden the heart," and "oil to make his face shine."

So, not only is it wine's purpose to bring joy, but this is its *God-intended purpose*. God created it for this very reason.

Indeed, God is a god of pleasure. He intends for His image to learn pleasure as well, and reflect His glory. Even that wild Leviathan sea monster was created for pleasure: "to play" (v. 26).

Drink Deeply, My Love

We have seen that God approves of (indeed, commanded) organized feasting with alcohol (Deut. 14:26), we have seen Jesus giving wine for others to enjoy, and we have seen several instances of biblical *shekar* ("intoxication") which in the good sense means enjoyment of an adequate amount of alcohol.

We should not be surprised, then, to see wine and "drunkenness" appear in God's definitive love poem, the Song of Solomon. Not only does it appear, it appears in a very striking way—so striking, that most translations are afraid to say it like it is. At least one is not:

> I came to my garden, my sister, my bride,
> I gathered my myrrh with my spice,

I ate my honeycomb with my honey,
I drank my wine with my milk.
Eat, friends, drink,
and be drunk with love! (Song 5:1 NAS).

Here is one of the erotic passages of the Song. The lover is entering his garden—the beloved—and eating her fruits, her honey, her milk, *and her wine*. And in the passion of intercourse the chorus arises, "Be drunk" (*shekar*) with love!

Here the intoxicating effect of alcohol serves as a poetic description of the effects of sexual passion. And boy, are they drunk with passionate love! The song describes their erotic thoughts in various places:

My beloved is mine, and I am his;
he grazes among the lilies.
Until the day breathes
and the shadows flee,
turn, my beloved, be like a gazelle
or a young stag on cleft mountains (Song 2:16–17).

The poem refers to her mountains more than once (2:17; 4:6, 8; 8:14), and it is not hard to understand what "cleft mountains" (or "mountains of cleavage") refers to; and thus it should not take much to imagine why she wants him to be like a stag, prancing upon the mountains all night until daybreak.

But just in case it is not clear, the lover tells us plainly:

Your two breasts are like two fawns,
twins of a gazelle,

that graze among the lilies.
Until the day breathes
and the shadows flee,
I will go away to the mountain of myrrh
and the hill of frankincense (4:5–6).

And she quickly responds,

Awake, O north wind,
and come, O south wind!
Blow upon my garden,
let its spices flow.
Let my beloved come to his garden,
and eat its choicest fruits (4:16).

Then follows the first passage quoted above, about the lover entering the garden.

Now no matter how you ultimately interpret the Song of Solomon (there are some competing views), they nevertheless must begin with the fact that it glorifies the enjoyment and even "drunkenness" of sexual love. And we should not be surprised at this, for God created male and female to be together (Gen. 2:21–25), and the marriage bed is undefiled (Heb. 13:4). What stands out clearly in the poem, however, is that sexuality is not presented as merely for procreation, but for passionate arousal and *enjoyment*:

As an apple tree among the trees of the forest,
so is my beloved among the young men.
With great delight I sat in his shadow,
and his fruit was sweet to my taste (Song 2:3).

My beloved put his hand to the latch,
and my heart was thrilled within me.
I arose to open to my beloved,
and my hands dripped with myrrh,
my fingers with liquid myrrh,
on the handles of the bolt (5:4–5).

In the end, all of the love poetry portrays Christ's love for His bride, the church. This love is compared in the Song to wine (1:2, 4; 4:10; 5:1; 7:9; 8:2) and the effects of alcohol (5:1; 7:9). It is not surprising, then, to see Christ at a wedding feast in Cana turning water into wine. Weddings feature in His parables (Matt. 22:2; 25:10; Luke 12:36). The very union of Christ to His church is called the marriage supper of the lamb (Rev. 19:7–9).

And practically every wedding in the whole Bible involves a feast (Gen. 29:22–25; Judg. 14:10–20; Matt. 22:1–14; 25:1–13; John 2:1–11; Rev. 19:7–9). The only exception is for Adam and Eve, and of course, there was no one else to invite anyway! But you can be sure they enjoyed each other.

God is a God of pleasure and joy. He has given us these great realities as images and symbols of His kingdom. It is no accident that the Lord's Supper, Holy Communion, has long since been called the "Eucharist"—which means, "thanksgiving." It is a feast, a feast of joy and thanks.

Christianity thanks God for His pleasures in glory. It thanks God for the foretaste of that bliss in this life—in the enjoyment of creation, of wine, of sex. Christianity is a religion of festival—of marriage feasts. It truly is a religion of wine, women, and song.

Veiling the Joy

While we know that sex can be abused, it would be entirely unbiblical to argue that since sex is so powerful, addictive, and potentially and often abused (to the ruin of many people and families), therefore we should ban women, or at least sex altogether. No, God created sex to be enjoyed within proper boundaries. The enjoyment of creation—wine, alcohol, etc.—is no different.

There is, however, a religion that is consistent in forbidding or suppressing both: *Islam*. Forbidding wine, women, and song, therefore, is something fundamentalists and prohibitionists have more in common with Islam than the Bible.

Muslims veil their women, demand total abstinence from wine, and allow no instrumental music. Notice the approach. Here is how Islam's Quran views wine:

> O ye who believe! wine and gambling and stone altars and divining arrows are only an abomination, a handiwork of Satan, shun it wherefore, that haply ye may fare well. Satan only seeketh to breed animosity and spites among you by means of wine and gambling and would keep you from the remembrance of Allah and from prayer; will ye not then desist? (Surah 5:89–90)

As a result of their satanic worldview, when Muslims captured Israel around AD 638, they destroyed all the vineyards that had been there for centuries—out of slavish fear of wine. Those thousands of winepresses which dripped God's blessings to His people harvest after harvest lay dry for the next twelve hundred years.[1]

As we have seen already, the Bible relates wine as a blessing, a joy, gladness, rest—all of which act as an earthly picture of God's future bliss for His people. We are called regularly to dine at the Lord's table with Him and drink His wine. In addition to this, we are encouraged periodically to feast and enjoy ourselves before Him.

And while the wine can be abused, we are not to forbid the picture of God's bliss for that reason—it is our remembrance of Him, and our memory of the future glorification and joy. Ironically, Islam has this exactly backwards: it forbids wine because, as it argues, it could cause us to forget God. Christianity invites us to receive of God's wine in order that we may frequently taste of the greater blessings to come.

Islam is a satanic perversion of Christianity. As such, it would have us forget God and His plan for man. When Christians forbid God's blessing of wine to other Christians, they are acting like Muslims instead of Christians.

---

1. http://www.prohibitionhangover.com/israelwine.html (accessed February 15, 2011).

Part 2:

⇒ *Fermentation* ⇐

Chapter 5

BOUNDARIES

You have heard it said, "Please drink responsibly." Even alcoholic beverage companies now include this type of admonition in their marketing and labeling. It's probably not a bad idea for them, either. It displays (whether they are conscious of it or not) a biblical view of drinking: one which encourages both enjoyment and moderation.

Wherever God gives liberty He also provides boundaries. For example, Adam and Eve could eat from any tree in the garden save one—the tree of the knowledge of good and evil. That tree was a line drawn in the sand. It was a test, yes: a test of their *faithfulness* to live according to God's boundaries. To have an entire world in which there was only one negative rule—"don't touch *this* tree"—is quite an amazing testimony to God's grace toward us. He created us fundamentally *free*.

Further, God created man in His image (Gen 1:26–30; 2:7). As God's image, man thinks God's thoughts and works God's works after Him (although on a smaller, finite scale). Just as God speaks, creates, names, governs, improves, and rests, so does His image engage in orderly communication, identifying, naming, (Gen. 2:18–25), governing (Gen. 1:28, Ps. 8:4–8), "creating" (building, making, manufacturing) and improving (Gen. 2:15), and resting (Gen. 2:2; Ex. 20:11). Man reflects the nature and purposes of his Creator.

Understandably then, when God first placed man in the garden, He did so for godly *purposes*: "The Lord God took the man and put him in the garden of Eden *to work it and keep it*" (Gen. 2:15). Man was to work the ground and to "keep" it, or "guard" it. His task was one of production and protection—that is, he was to guard its boundaries.

Of course, Adam and Eve crossed God's sole boundary—they ate from the forbidden tree. They immediately learned a hard lesson about boundaries. God kicked them out of Eden and placed a "no-trespassing" sign at the gate—an angel with a sword of fire. "Do not cross this line."

It's interesting that we still often speak of sin today as "trespassing."

There are, then, basically two types of boundaries. *First*, God's ethical boundaries. These are things that God specifically says not to do. Sometimes we don't fully understand *why*, but God simply reveals them. Things like, "Don't eat from that tree." We may be tempted to ask why not, seeing that by appearances *that* tree looks no different than any other (and it's a *victimless crime*, some may rationalize), but it doesn't matter: God said "No."

Second, there are God's natural boundaries. These are God's built-in limits in the natural world. For example, you could genetically modify certain types of grapes to withstand certain diseases and pests. But you can't create grape vines that are genetically modified to withstand a bulldozer. There are certain limits on what you can and cannot do in the natural world.

Alcohol involves both types of boundaries. There is only so much alcohol an individual can consume before enjoyment cedes to inebriation, and then sickness. One can die from alcohol poisoning. On top of this natural limit, God has decreed an ethical limit. Indulging oneself to the point of such inebriation—we commonly call it "drunkenness"—is an infraction of God's right way of living. Thus, drunkenness trespasses both kinds of boundaries—it defies God in both His created order and His revealed Word.

It should go without saying in any Christian discussion of the use of alcohol—at least, any discussion that honors Scripture as God's Word—that *drunkenness*, excess, or *abuse* of wine is detestable to God and clearly a sin. Whether on the conservative side of the Christian spectrum (like me) or on the more liberal side—heck, even liberals who deny the inspiration and truth of Scripture—*all* parties would acknowledge that the Bible forbids and condemns drunkenness. Liberals would probably be more likely to make mainly social and pragmatic arguments against it, however, whereas some fearful and misguided believers like to extend God's condemnation of *abuse* into a blanket prohibition on *use*.

While I think I have shown in the preceding chapters why a prohibitionist view is terribly awry, we would do well to stop and reiterate the Bible's teaching on the abuse of alcohol. We'll do this for two reasons: 1) it makes up an important and substantial part of the Bible's overall teaching on alcohol, and 2) I hope to deflect the age-old and long-tired criticism that by advocating and glorifying the *use* of alcohol, Christians like me downplay the dangers of abuse and/or encourage many Christians to get drunk and fall into ruinous sin.

Seven Woes[1]

I will state the biblical case against drunkenness succinctly. Honestly, it is so clear it does not need much more elucidation than this.

First, drunkenness is a rejection of God's created reality. Proverbs 23:29–35 and Isaiah 28:7 describe a drunkard: he sees strange things, rambles, loses his orientation, staggers, and becomes numb even to a beating. Yet he seeks the wine again afterwards. This involves (among other things) a problem of escapism—altering and numbing one's experience of God's creation in order not to deal with stress, problems, responsibility, etc. Considering the theology we learned earlier, this type of denial equals the making of an idol. The drunkard has passed the point of God's blessing in the little taste of bliss found in alcohol, and has pursued the fullness of that bliss in the earthly creature (See also Is. 56:12). This is idolatry.

Second, drunkenness makes you socially revolting. You lose self-control of both your body and behavior. The result can include things like tables "full of filthy vomit, with no space left" (Is. 28:8), staggering (Is. 28:7), staggering *in* one's own vomit (Is. 19:14), falling and passing out (Jer. 25:27), arguing and complaining (Prov. 23:29),

---

1. I have adapted the following seven points from Gentry's more detailed covering of them in his *God Gave Wine*, 17–32. He provided eight points; I have consolidated two and so present seven. I recommend Gentry's scholarly study for a more in-depth treatment.

loud-mouthing and rowdiness (Prov. 20:1), fighting (Prov. 23:35), sexual exploitation (Hab. 2:15–16). This is hardly fitting of a Christian who is supposed to exhibit the fruit of the Spirit, including self-control (Gal. 5:22–3), and do nothing to offend (1 Cor. 10:32; 2 Cor. 6:3; Phil. 1:10).

Third, drunkenness deteriorates the body. It is bad enough to lose self-control, but many suffer sickness, weakness, disorder, and even disease because of alcohol abuse. Chronic alcoholism can not only shorten your life and wrack your body with pain, it can also rob you of ever enjoying alcohol in moderation again. Recovered alcoholics will often avoid the substance altogether for fear of falling into abuse once again. Sometimes, when we abuse God's gifts, He takes them away for good, and with much sorrow, fear, and regret. And guys, it is a well-known medical fact that excessive alcohol can shrink your testicles, and destroy sperm count.

Fourth, drunkenness perverts and corrupts moral judgment. Hosea 4:11 says that whoredom, wine and "new wine" can "take away the understanding." Just as you can get physically numb, you will also lose moral sensitivity. For example, Lot's daughters got their father drunk until he slept with them (Gen. 19:32). Paul finds drunkenness accompanying things like "sexual immorality, impurity, sensuality, idolatry, sorcery, enmity, strife, jealousy, fits of anger, rivalries, dissensions, divisions, envy . . . orgies, and things like these" (Gal. 5:19–21).

As such, and *fifth*, drunkenness destroys vocational capacity. Whereas God originally created us for dominion, productivity, and purpose (Gen 1:28; Ps. 8:4–8), drunkenness represents distraction, escapism, waste, and carelessness. Such a state can only detract and diminish—if not destroy—your work and all constructive judgment on top of your moral judgment. For these reasons among others, God forbid priests or Levites from imbibing alcohol while performing their duties (Lev. 10:8–9; Ezek. 44:21). The same rule applied to civil rulers in their capacity, for they could forget the law and pervert justice (Prov. 31:4–5). In all jobs and callings, Solomon warns that drunkenness and gluttony will lead to poverty (23:20).

For all these reasons, and *sixth*, drunkenness is often a manifestation of God's judgment on society. Drunkenness often provides a metaphor for the deranged society that will suffer under God's cursing (Ezek. 23:28–33; Lam. 4:21–22). Sometimes it is listed as a cause for judgment, whether literally or metaphorically (Is. 28:7, Rev. 17–18). God will also use literal drunkenness as a curse in the leadership of a rebellious society:

> Then you shall say to them, "Thus says the Lord: Behold, I will fill with drunkenness all the inhabitants of this land: the kings who sit on David's throne, the priests, the prophets, and all the inhabitants of Jerusalem. And I will dash them one against another, fathers and sons together, declares the Lord. I will not pity or spare or have compassion, that I should not destroy them" (Jer. 13:13–14).

Of course, it could all be stated even more briefly and simply than these succinct points. For lastly, drunkenness is openly, clearly, and directly forbidden in Scripture:

Wine is a mocker, strong drink a brawler, and whoever is led astray by it is not wise (Prov. 20:1).

And do not get drunk with wine, for that is debauchery, but be filled with the Spirit (Eph. 5:18).

Now the works of the flesh are evident: sexual immorality, impurity, sensuality, idolatry, sorcery, enmity, strife, jealousy, fits of anger, rivalries, dissensions, divisions, envy, drunkenness, orgies, and things like these. I warn you, as I warned you before, that those who do such things will not inherit the kingdom of God (Gal. 5:19–21; cf. 1 Cor. 6:10).

Jesus Himself warned His disciples that drunkenness would dull their watchfulness: "But watch yourselves lest your hearts be weighed down with dissipation and drunkenness and cares of this life, and that day come upon you suddenly like a trap" (Luke 21:34). Considering that Jesus here was warning them to be watchful for the coming destruction of Jerusalem (Luke 21:5–7), being oblivious through drunkenness could certainly have cost the disciples their lives.

For these seven reasons and probably more, Scripture clearly condemns drunkenness as a sin and a curse upon mankind.

Yet even considering the horrible potential of wine and strong drink, God nowhere forbids enjoyment of them, only the abuse.

An Interesting Comparison

While there is a near obsession with some pastors and other Christians to denounce all alcohol use as abuse and sin, it is instructive to compare this phenomenon with the near silence concerning the outright abuse of very similar bodily enjoyments. This problem has two parts: the frequency of the preaching on these topics, and the fallacy of how alcohol is treated in comparison.

First, consider the frequency. I can personally attest that among the thousands of sermons I've heard (not counting the many I daydreamed or slept through), I have heard alcohol mentioned and denounced many, many times as a "don't touch this" sin. I have, in fact, heard entire sermons devoted to the topic. In comparison, I have not heard gluttony, for example, preached against more than twice that I can remember. Why not? Scripture often enjoins drunkenness and gluttony together (Deut. 21:20; Prov. 23:21; Matt. 11:19; Luke 7:34). Why do preachers give so much emphasis to the one and not the other?

Considering the rotundity of some of the preachers I remember railing against raising a glass, perhaps preaching on alcohol helped distract them from the topic of their own addictive sin. There's nothing like diverting attention from your sin by bellowing about someone else's. For some of the guys I've seen in pulpits, "pass the plate" has meaning beyond just tithes and offerings. But unfortunately, both drunkenness and gluttony are equally bad and revolting sins.

They say, "But alcohol has such terrible effects." Yes it can. But so does overeating. Nearly ten percent of medical costs in the U.S. derive from the overweight and obese. Medical costs directly related to these tally $147 billion per year.[2] That's because overeating can lead to the following health risks: high blood pressure, high cholesterol, cardiovascular disease, high triglycerides, type 2 diabetes, breathing problems, sleep apnea, gallbladder disease, joint and cartilage deterioration, arthritis, increased risk of stroke, increased risk of endometrial, breast, and colon cancer, and higher risk of infertility. And while not all obesity results merely from overeating, at least one scientific study has blamed the modern trend of increasing obesity entirely on gluttony.[3]

Further, obese individuals are less likely to be hired and likely to be paid less when hired. Total economic costs, including loss of work and productivity due to these conditions totals $270 billion.[4]

Not to mention, some airlines charge the obese for two seats.

Secondly, consider the logic of the "no alcohol at all" view. It is ridiculous to argue that just because something *can* be abused, therefore we should disallow it completely. The bad usage of a good thing is no reason to throw out the good thing. Follow the same logic, for example, with the sin we just covered: Food can be abused (glut-

2.   http://abcnews.go.com/Health/Healthday/story?id=8184975&page=1

3.   http://www.webmd.com/diet/news/20090511/obesity-epidemic-overeating-alone-to-blame

4.   http://www.usatoday.com/yourlife/health/medical/2011-01-12-obesity-costs-300-bilion_N.htm

tony). Should we therefore forbid all food? Sex can be abused (adultery, fornication, pornography, etc.). Should we therefore forbid all sex? This is what Roman Catholics have done for their priests. Perhaps the "don't even touch wine" fundamentalists should all become monks as well.

Anything can be abused. Heck, my grandpa told me many years ago that you can drink too much water. I asked, "What will happen?" The old farmer replied, "Well, you'll just conk out!" I had to laugh. But he was right:

> Water poisoning . . . is a potentially fatal disturbance in brain functions that results when the normal balance of electrolytes in the body is pushed outside of safe limits by over-consumption of water.[5]

Conclusion

God's boundaries apply to all of human experience. You can eat or drink to excess of any substance. Just because you can abuse a substance does not mean you should refuse it totally. This applies to alcohol as much as to any food or drink.

Yet we must always honor the boundaries.

---

5.   http://en.wikipedia.org/wiki/Water_intoxication

Chapter 6

FERMENTING FEAR

Anytime a Christian wishes to condemn alcohol in any way, it seems they always end up quoting Proverbs 23:31. It says, "Do not look at wine when it is red, when it sparkles in the cup and goes down smoothly." The passage goes on to warn of its dangerous outcome: "In the end it bites like a serpent and stings like an adder" (v. 32). It is very clear that there is a solemn warning here.

According to the teetotaler, this verse tells us to abstain from wine, "when it is red." These people almost always argue that this is a reference to fermentation. We will see some examples of preachers who say this later. For now, suffice it to say that this is the standard "proof-text" for avoiding not only drunkenness, but even tasting all fermented beverages altogether.

Before we address this particular interpretation of this one verse, we need to look at the whole context. As the wise preacher once said, "A proof-text without a context becomes a pretext." This is exactly what we find with Proverbs 23:31.

Ruling Lusts

In reality, the whole of chapter 23 is the proper context. Apart from that, verse 31 will almost certainly be misunderstood and misapplied. The theme of the whole chapter is the dangers of lust. As most of the book of Proverbs teaches, lust leads to foolishness, whereas self-control is a fruit of wisdom. This theme is introduced at the very start of the chapter:

> When you sit down to eat with a ruler, observe carefully what is before you, and put a knife to your throat if you are given to appetite. Do not desire his delicacies, for they are deceptive food. . . . Do not eat the bread of an evil eye; do not lust after his delicacies, for he is like one who is inwardly calculating. "Eat and drink!" he says to you, but his heart is not with you (Prov. 23:1–3, 6–7).[1]

The key phrase here is "given to appetite." "Given" means completely given over to—totally invested in. The Hebrew literally means something closer to "ruled by appetite." This is not about the food and drink itself, it is about an absence of self-control.

The situation here is a microcosm of human life: there are lusts to be avoided, for lusts pervert judgment and lead to destruction. The devil places all types of temptations in front of us, hoping we will lust after them and bite (or drink). Politicians—the devil's nearest counterpart on earth—use the exact same tactics. So do lobbyists: wine and dine and bring in the prostitutes. As one debauched California politician of the 1970s said, "If you can't eat their food, drink their booze, screw their women and then vote against them, you have no business being up here." If you are the type of person who cannot say no, then you might as well not even show up

1. I have used some of my own translation here, based mostly on the ESV.

to the table—you will lose the negotiations and eventually everything else.

The main theme is plainly reiterated in verses 20–21: "Be not among drunkards or among gluttonous eaters of meat, for the drunkard and the glutton will come to poverty, and slumber will clothe them with rags."

Notice that the Proverb does not forbid the "delicacies" or wine or meat altogether. It does not even condemn them in themselves at all. The warning, rather, is about two things: 1) an *uncontrolled* appetite, and 2) the evil intentions of the tempter. Be warned of both.

Now the entire chapter 23 goes on to elaborate this theme in many examples, highlighting different things upon which our lusts can focus. Without going through a complete exposition, here is the short version: beware of your soul being ruled by food (vv. 1–3, 6–7), riches and wealth (vv. 4–5), an audience (v. 9), envy (v. 17), sex (vv. 27–28), and finally, wine (vv. 29–35).

Overcoming Satan's devices requires discipline. Discipline is self-control. Self-control is wise. This is highlighted clearly in the middle of the chapter: "Buy truth, and do not sell it; buy wisdom, instruction, and understanding" (v. 23). We are told also to instill this in our children when they are young. Sin leads to painful correction, but discipline saves you from perishing: "Do not withhold discipline from a child; if you strike him with a rod, he will not die. If you strike him with the rod, you will save his soul from Sheol" (vv. 13–14).

It is clear then that we should view the section of this Proverb that deals with wine as teaching the same theme that the rest of the chapter teaches: do not lose control because of the seductive nature of the things of this world. This includes the alluring nature of wine.

This helps us understand the nature of the passage on wine. Since the theme involves how the devil tries to tempt undisciplined people into excesses by seducing them, we should understand the passage on wine as a poetic description of how wine appears to someone whose appetite has already put them under its spell: "Do not look at wine when it is red, when it sparkles in the cup and goes down smoothly." To the person ruled by this lust, the color of wine, the sparkle in the cup, and the thought of that flavor flowing down the throat like velvet completely overwhelm the senses—and the person is then ruled by that appetite.

The person sitting at the king's table, given to appetite, should "put a knife to the throat." Not literally, of course, but simply do whatever it takes to restrain himself from falling prey. Similarly, the drinker, faced with that smooth sparkling drink awaiting in that cup, should do whatever it takes to control the situation. If the senses are overwhelmed, if you will have no control, then remove the sensory overload: "Do not look."

Whatever one may teach about this specific verse in itself, it is clear that the whole chapter goes together. So, if we make the mistake of thinking verse 31 absolutely forbids alcohol, then this mentality should apply to all the other potential abuses in the chapter. If we must totally abstain from alcohol in this passage, then we must also totally abstain from all food, all money, all talking, and all sex, for these also can be addictive and through abuse can easily become sin.

For those who see this consistent application of the prohibitive interpretation as producing a somewhat poor quality of life, then let them learn the lesson of the chapter: beware of the power of lust to lead you into poor decisions. Learn self-control and apply it to your life. This applies to drinking wine, and to every other area of life as well.

Once you embrace a life of self-control, you will be on the road to maturity. A mature Christian knows how to enjoy God's gifts without absolute fear of them, and yet also knows when and where to stop.

Fermented Translation

Once we understand that this verse is poetry about seduction, then we are in a better position to address those who abuse the passage. According to most anti-alcohol interpretations, Prov. 23:31 refers to the process of fermentation, and thus it means there's a clear distinction in the Bible between "wine" that is fresh and wine that is "red," or fermented.

First of all, as we saw in chapter 2, the Hebrew language has words that refer to freshly squeezed grape juice. God could easily have used these if he intended to talk about grape juice most of the time. The Bible barely uses these words at all. It is more honest to acknowledge that alcoholic wine is the biblical norm.

Secondly, on what basis do the teetotaling preachers say that this verse refers to fermentation? The common argument is based upon the King James Version: "Look not thou upon the wine when it is red, when it giveth his colour in the cup, when it moveth itself aright." The argument says that the wine here has changed color and is moving itself. The change in color is supposedly caused by fermentation, and in the process of fermentation the wine releases bubbles (as we discussed previously) and could create a stirring within the vat. The wine thus "moves itself."

Unfortunately, most of this is based on a poor translation. Admittedly, the Hebrew is difficult here (as the poetry sections often are), but hardly any other English translation follows the erroneous King James on this passage. Here are just a couple of points at which it is really bad: the phrase "giveth his colour" literally means "gives its eye." The word for "eye" never refers to color in Hebrew. In this case it likely refers to something about wine in the glass that catches the eye. Almost all modern English translations call it "sparkle." The other bad phrase is "moveth itself aright." The modern English attempts are better: they almost all say something like, "goes down smoothly." Even the old Geneva Bible says "goeth down pleasantly," and this was translated fifty years before the King James!

The better translation helps clarify the meaning. The wine is not moving itself in the sense that it is acting upon itself, stirring itself up. Rather, it is moving itself smoothly from the cup and down the throat. The redness, the sparkle, and the smoothness are not signifying that some change has taken place in the juice itself, but rather are the basic characteristics of wine that allure people who love wine.

The ESV is accuratein its translation: "Do not look at wine when it is red, when it sparkles in the cup and goes down smoothly." Ironically, as much as I despise the modern paraphrase translations, I actually think *The Message* captures the point well: "Don't judge wine by its label, or its bouquet, or its full-bodied flavor." The point is to highlight the qualities of wine which draw people to it, not to give criteria for distinguishing the process of fermentation.

This understanding fits properly into the overall context. It clearly indicates the being ruled by wine is a sin, but this has nothing to do with the mere act of drinking a fermented beverage. Anyone who continues to impose the "Don't touch alcohol" belief based on this verse shows that they have no idea what Proverbs 23 is about, have no knowledge at all how to handle biblical languages (and probably don't care to learn), and believe more in controlling people with fear than with wisdom, understanding, and self-discipline.

Be Not Drunk With Wine

The emphasis here is not on grape juice versus wine, but upon exercising self-control, and avoiding excess. For this reason the larger passage (vv. 29–35) is a picture of the effects of drunkenness. We are given a keen insight into the drunkard's world:

> Who has woe? Who has sorrow? Who has strife? Who has complaining? Who has wounds without cause? Who has redness of eyes? Those who tarry long over wine; those who go to try mixed wine. Do

not look at wine when it is red, when it sparkles in the cup and goes down smoothly. In the end it bites like a serpent and stings like an adder. Your eyes will see strange things, and your heart utter perverse things. You will be like one who lies down in the midst of the sea, like one who lies on the top of a mast. "They struck me," you will say, "but I was not hurt; they beat me, but I did not feel it. When shall I awake? I must have another drink" (Prov. 23:29–35).

Several things about this further support the interpretation given so far. The person to whom the redness, sparkle, and smoothness greatly appeal is not just anyone and everyone, but rather the person accustomed to "tarry long" over wine, and who will "got to" or "search for" wine. This person is already ruled by wine in his heart. Even after this person has wasted himself once again, passed out, was beaten, and was numb to everything, he turns again: "I must have another drink."

The issue here is not the act of consumption, but the total loss of control. The issue is not drinking, but drunkenness.

This is supported further by Paul's use of this passage. Most readers are not aware that Paul actually quotes Proverbs 23:31 in his letter to the Ephesians. We are not quick to catch it because he quotes a version of the Old Testament that we are unfamiliar with—the Greek translation done around 250 BC, called the Septuagint. It is not always as accurate as we would like but it is very often helpful in seeing what Greek terms the ancient theologians used to translate Old Testament Hebrew ideas.

Thus we can learn quite a bit about the New Testament through this means. Indeed, many times when the New Testament authors quote the Old Testament, they're quoting the Greek Septuagint rather than the Hebrew texts, because Greek was more widely known throughout the world at the time. Paul quotes from it often.

One such place is very interesting. In a well-known passage of Paul, he says, "Do not get drunk with wine, for that is debauchery, but be filled with the Spirit. . . ." (Eph. 5:18). The irony here is that this is a direct quotation (in the Greek) of the Septuagint version of Proverbs 23:31! In other words, the Greek version of the Old Testament translates Prov. 23:31 to mean something more than just looking at, touching, or merely drinking wine; it means full-blown drunkenness. This is the version Paul chose to quote. This means that Paul understood Proverbs 23:31 to be speaking about drunkenness—excess—and not merely drinking wine in and of itself.

Chapter 7

ABOUT THE WEAKER
BROTHER

Many Christians take what appears to be a compromising position on the subject of alcohol. Acknowledging the Bible's clear position on the subject, they refuse to take the ridiculous line of forbidding all alcohol. Good so far. But then, caving under who knows what social and/or religious pressures—and there are many—they then argue that Christians should voluntary abstain from alcohol.

This devious moral swindle is the *back door* to prohibition. While not formally forbidding alcohol, it *practically* forbids it. Under the guise of freedom they forbid. Giving permission, they prohibit. This view pays little more than lip service to God's revealed will, but has little intention of growing to maturity in it.

In many (perhaps most) cases, the people advancing this argument come from some variety of a prohibitionist background (it could be Baptist, Pentecostal, Charismatic, Methodist, or many others). The audiences to which they minister still retain many vestiges of the old ways of thinking; thus certain ministers and teachers in these traditions—although they are trained better in what the Bible actually says—must still bow to the social pressures that demonize alcohol.

In other cases, where people may not have come out of these traditions personally, they may have been influenced by them in other ways—perhaps by attending a seminary saturated with that tradition, or simply by being hired to preach or teach in such a church. The social and traditional pressures are ever-present, even for those many modern-day churches that claim to spurn "tradition" (indeed, hating "tradition" in many churches today has itself become a tradition).

To support their double-mindedness, these teachers will turn primarily to two passages of Scripture: 1) Paul's distinction between "lawful . . . but not helpful" (1 Cor. 6:12), and 2) Paul's teaching on the weaker brother (Rom. 14–15). These two often are intertwined, but are always misunderstood and thus misapplied. Let us take a closer look at these two passages.

Lawful and Helpful

These backdoor prohibitionists remind us that Paul said "'All things are lawful for me,' but not all things are helpful. 'All things are lawful for me,' but I will not be enslaved by anything" (1 Cor. 6:12). By this reference we are expected to make the analogy: "Drinking alcohol is lawful, but not helpful. It is lawful, but I will not be enslaved by it."

In order to enforce this application, they will then pour out streams of evidence that alcohol has bad effects on society, or can *possibly* have bad effects for the Christian. One of those trendy megachurches recently posted a video version of this argument on YouTube as their answer to Christians and alcohol.[1] It displays how fallacious this slippery slope can get.

The production portrays a campus pastors' conference where several young pastors with cool hair and cool t-shirts are enjoying themselves poolside. One decides to have a beer he finds in a cooler. The minute he pops the top, the others scream "Beer party," and suddenly coolers of beer are carried in. Within minutes the party is drunk, loud, and out of control. A policeman shows up due to the noise; while he's there a fight breaks out and a brawling, drunken pastor ends up scuffling, unsuccessfully, with the cop. He is cuffed and goes to jail. Lesson 1: even one beer will lead to huge problems. Lesson 2: drinking may be lawful, but is definitely not beneficial.

Now what's wrong with this picture? *First*, obviously these idiots have zero self-control (as we talked about in Proverbs 23). The moment the beer was opened, they lost it (they hadn't even drunk any yet!). As such, they have no Christian maturity and should never have made it into the pastorate. They are hardly representative of how any Christian should behave, period.

Second, these guys drank directly to excess. Again, zero self-control, zero maturity. They have no idea what alcohol is for, biblically, or how to handle it. Having one drink, or even a few in your home, *never* automatically means that you will of necessity drink to excess. This is nonsense: treating a remote possibility as a likelihood, let alone an inevitability. The radical degree of comic farce

---

1. http://www.youtube.com/watch?v=f0SrnsaGMHA (accessed, February 15, 2011).

involved here is really an argument for alcohol consumption rather than against it.

Third, any pastor with judgment so poor—even after consuming alcohol—as to come to blows with a brother and defy law enforcement, again, has no business ever being in that position. The qualifications for elder require the individual to be "not a drunkard, not violent but gentle, not quarrelsome" (1 Tim. 3:3). It is ridiculous to use a man of such low caliber to portray a model Christian in such a scenario. A group of model Christians, certainly pastors, would have all enjoyed alcohol within the limits of Christian maturity and self-control. No cop would have even shown up. No problem. God is glorified in our enjoyment of His blessings and community.

The very fact that this scenario *could possibly* have happened is ridiculous. Any one of those pastors could be portrayed making *any* mistake, and then that mistake used as a lever to forbid any type of behavior. This is classic fallacious slippery-slope argumentation: it leverages fear of what might happen rather than promoting maturity and responsibility.

Besides, the qualifications for elders also require that they be "not a lover of money" (1 Tim. 3:3). Since money in itself can possibly lead one to become a "lover of money" (covetous), should we therefore abstain from it totally? Yet, I don't see any of these pastors preaching "money is lawful, but not beneficial." Does a single one refuse his paycheck because of what might possibly happen to him spiritually? Can you now see why this type of argument is a fallacy when applied to alcohol as well?

To what, then, does the verse in 1 Corinthian 6 really refer? What is the context? From verse 9 through the end of the chapter, Paul is dealing with things that are *clearly excess and clearly forbidden sins*. He is not using the argument "all things are lawful," he is debunking it. After all, this passage is preceded by Paul teaching,

> Do you not know that the unrighteous will not inherit the kingdom of God? Do not be deceived: neither the sexually immoral, nor idolaters, nor adulterers, nor men who practice homosexuality, nor thieves, nor the greedy, nor drunkards, nor revilers, nor swindlers will inherit the kingdom of God.

Obviously, not all things are "lawful." Many behaviors will keep you out of the kingdom. In verses 13–20, Paul deals with prostitution—it's obviously not allowed in the Christian life. When Paul addresses the saying again in chapter 10 verse 23 of the same book, the issue is now idolatry—eating meat sacrificed to idols. None of the sins involved here are an issue of being lawful for the Christian yet merely "unprofitable," or "not helpful." These sins are sins that are transgressions of the law of God whatever word you choose to call that law.

In short, Paul is refuting antinomianism—the view that Christians have no law as a guide to their living, and thus are free to do whatever as long as they "believe." This "lawful but not helpful" passage, therefore, does not apply to the practical issues of areas in which God has clearly already given us freedom, it applies to the false belief that God has given us freedom in *every* area.

But this is never to deny that God indeed *has* given us freedom in many areas, not the least of which is in the enjoyment of alcohol.

That the saying "but not helpful" should not be used as a guide for determining behaviors that God has already qualified as free strengthens when we see Paul apply it to himself—and then *ignore it*. In 2 Corinthians 12:1, Paul begins a passage about his experience of being caught up to "the third heaven," receiving unutterable revelations from God, and then being given a "thorn in the flesh" to keep Him humble. Paul begins this mysterious passage by saying this: "I must go on boasting. Though there is nothing to be gained by it, I will go on to visions and revelations of the Lord." The phrase "there is nothing to be gained by it," is the equivalent Greek phrase to "not all things are helpful" (1 Cor. 6:12). Boasting about his experiences, in other words, was lawful but not helpful—yet Paul did it anyway. Why? Because, first, "lawful but not helpful" *is not a binding guide to Christian freedom to begin with*; and second, because there was a deeper lesson to be learned through the humility that came with Paul's reason for boasting. There was a level of maturity to which the Corinthians needed to advance.

While I have hardly said all that could be said about the misuse of this passage and its attendant fallacies, I hope you can see already how misguided it is. It is an argument of fear, masquerading as charity. It creates a back door to let in the very prohibition these guys know the Bible does not teach. It's a way of using the Bible to ignore the Bible.

The Weaker Brother

If the prohibitionist refuses Christian maturity under the guise of Christian purity, the "weaker brother" argument refuses maturity under the guise of charity. While this is true, also, of the "lawful but not helpful" group, it is even more egregious with the "weaker brother" clan.

This group reminds us that, again, while the Bible certainly does not condemn enjoying alcohol in and of itself, it nevertheless provides a crippling hurdle to doing so in the fear that we may offend this character called "the weaker brother." This lesson comes from Paul's teaching to the Romans: "It is good not to eat meat or drink wine or do anything that causes your brother to stumble" (Rom. 14:21). This verse is then interpreted to mean that if any other Christian is offended by you drinking wine, then you should abstain. This seems to gain legitimacy from the context: "For if your brother is grieved by what you eat, you are no longer walking in love" (v. 15).

Sometimes, the passage is applied to those who struggle with alcoholism, because drinking in a social setting may tempt such a brother to fall back into his addiction. There is legitimacy here, and I will deal with it in a moment. For now, we must consider how this applies in normal situations between otherwise healthy Christians.

Again, we must consider the whole context. The entirety of Romans 14 deals with how to admit brethren "weak in the faith." The opening of the chapter is instructive:

> As for the one who is weak in faith, welcome him, but not to quarrel over opinions. One person be-

lieves he may eat anything, while the weak person eats only vegetables. Let not the one who eats
despise the one who abstains, and let not the one
who abstains pass judgment on the one who eats,
for God has welcomed him. Who are you to pass
judgment on the servant of another? It is before
his own master that he stands or falls. And he will
be upheld, for the Lord is able to make him stand
(Rom. 14:1–5).

What do we learn from this passage?

First, Paul treats the weaker brother as the outsider.
He is not running the show; he is to be received by the
stronger in faith. He is obviously, therefore not in a position of leadership in the church.

Second, "weak" or "strong" is a measurement of one's
beliefs in freedom. The strong believes in more freedom,
the weak believes in less. Therefore:

Third, the weak brother is the one who *forbids*. He is
the one who believes in forbidding certain substances or
practices: for example, eating meat, drinking wine, ob-
serving festivals, etc. In other words, drinking wine is
not considered a departure from the faith, but rather an
dexpression of *strong* faith. It is the prohibitionists and
the abstainers who are considered weak.

Fourth, the rule of charity requires *both* parties to allow the other to practice freely: "Let not the one who eats
despise the one who abstains, and let not the one who
abstains pass judgment on the one who eats" (14:3). If the
prohibitionist publicly demands that others abstain as
well, then he is transgressing the love of the brethren. He

is forsaking "righteousness and peace and joy in the Holy Spirit" (v. 17). He is at fault, not the drinker.

From these considerations, Paul examines the role of the stronger. Since they are stronger, they should be able to bear the weaknesses of the weak (Rom. 15:1). But this does not mean that the weak are to be catered to in every way and at all times. If so, the whole church would have to be structured and operated according to the weakness of the weakest member. It would rule out all teaching and persuasion towards stronger faith and maturity—for this would conflict with that member's weak faith and thereby offend him. No, the weaker is to be received with the *mutual understanding* that whatever the issue is, it will not be made a criteria for judging each other in the church. It will rather be left to private considerations, and left there.

Remember, Paul's original example is of a brother who eats all things compared to a weak brother who is a vegetarian (14:2). Do you have a single vegetarian in your church? By the argument of the weaker brother clan, therefore, the entire church must never do anything to offend the vegetarian faithful. This means veggie-only potlucks, veggie-only church picnics and events, etc. Is this really what Paul means in this verse? Is the weakness of the weakest brother really supposed to become the operating norm for the whole church?

The final verse is instructive as well: "But whoever has doubts is condemned if he eats, because the eating is not from faith. For whatever does not proceed from faith is sin" (14:23). If you pressure someone into doing the opposite of what they believe, then you have crossed Paul's line. If someone honestly believes in abstaining, then let them abstain. But this does not give them the right to make it an issue in the church, to quarrel with others about it, or to lord abstinence over those who partake. Yet it also does not give the stronger brethren the right to belittle him or push him out of the fellowship. Each should practice their faith freely in matters that are not fundamental to the faith: "The faith that you have, keep between yourself and God" (v. 22).

So it is not helpful or biblical to use the "weaker brother" passages to try to force others to abstain. This breaks the very rule the passage is teaching. To do so is, again, to promote fear in place of charity, and prevents the rest of the church from moving on to maturity and joy.

A Serious Situation

With all of this said, and as much as I personally defend and uphold the Christian's right to enjoy wine, beer, and spirits, let me add a warning to temper the mood. If you have ever experienced anyone struggling with the demons of alcoholism, you'll understand this point. Christians should never flaunt this liberty or make these arguments flippantly (this is certainly part of what Paul was confronting in 1 Corinthians—the flaunting of liberty to the crushing of others). Alcoholism emaciates once strong men, cripples lives, destroys marriages, shreds friendships, ends jobs, ends careers, and ends lives. It is a serious and very sad business. No one enjoying themselves in any social setting that tempts a recovering alcoholic to drink again can be said to be acting in a spirit of Christian love. It's simply selfish and irresponsible. When we say "Please drink responsibly," it refers to more than whether you will be driving. It refers to more than the volume of alcohol. Sometimes it does mean having none at all for the sake of your brother. If you're not responsible enough to make that call for him, then you're probably not responsible enough to drink for yourself either.

I take a keen lesson from Dr. John Piper, who personally abstains from alcohol, but who shares the proper biblical view: "Of course you can't defend in any absolute way teetotalism from the Bible. It's clear that wine is a blessing in the Bible." Yet, having spent many painful hours speaking, counseling, and praying with Christians struggling with the effects of alcoholism, he gives a passionate plea for Christians to have compassion in the face of it. He adds, "People who are cavalier about this thing called alcohol make no sense to me."[2] I agree. It's just as sinful to ignore real suffering and danger as it is to deny God's blessing in the substance.

---

2. See http://www.youtube.com/watch?v=MMKbTOgp69o.

Part 3:

═ *Sour Grapes* ═

Chapter 8

DRUNKSCHATOLOGY

Drunkschatology is not one of the traditional branches of theology. I admit, I made it up. But being a trained theologian, I have a warrant to make things up. Considering how many centuries monks have been making beer and wine, however, I am surprised another theologian has not beat me to this.

I made up the word by cramming together the two words "drunk" and "eschatology."

Eschatology is the branch of theology that studies "last things" (from the Greek *eschatos*, "last," and *logos*, "study"). Most popularly this study focuses on Bible prophecy, end times, and things like that. Thus it can also simply describe the study of how God's promises have come to pass throughout history, and this affects how *we* view the future based on God's promises.

The Bible warns us and teaches us a lot about how a false worldview can create many other problems in our Christian life. I have already discussed some of the biblical theology of wine and how it symbolizes a glorious kingdom of blessing to come. There are, however, two main perversions of this view: the one that indulges in the wine itself, and the one that harshly forbids it. The one ignores the faithfulness of God's promises, the other ignores the goodness of His creation.

Each of these is a type of excess—the one ignoring God's boundaries, the other ignoring His blessings.

Each creates an allegiance beyond God's Word—the one totally ruled by the substance, the other totally afraid of it. By "drunkschatology" then, I intend to show the idolatrous worldview of the drunkard, and its sister-sin—the damaging worldview of those who overreact in the opposite way.

Most systematic theologies do not include a section on the drunk's worldview, and this is a shame. The drunk has more to teach us about fallen man's spirituality than most theologians have heretofore given him credit. He has a type of wisdom all his own. I think that just as C. S. Lewis taught us about human folly and Christian living by studying the wiles of the devil (remember *The Screwtape Letters*?), so could we learn many valuable things about human nature from that most pervasive of sins, excess.

Drunk Eschatology

Isaiah 56:12 reveals the drunkard's skewed view of the future. He thinks he can escape into the oblivion of drunkenness, and when he returns, he only has to do it again for more bliss. Only he thinks—against all common sense—that the next time will be even better:

> "Come," they say, "let me get wine; let us fill ourselves with strong drink; and tomorrow will be like this day, great beyond measure."

This is the Bible's warning that alcohol is addictive, and that as people are sucked into that addiction, they lose reality a little more every time. This is the drunkenness condemned in the Bible: habitual drunkenness. This is making the liquor an idol and letting it have control over you.

But considering idolatry, alcohol is no worse than any other idol. Perhaps it is worse in the fact that it adds a physical addiction to spiritual idolatry, but that is true of *all* addictions, including food, sex, tobacco, drugs, video games, gambling, laziness, hoarding, shopping, ESPN, romance novels, *ad infinitum.*

In each case, the person given to addiction is seeking to extend the enjoyment they get from the first experience into future experiences. But addictions always require a little more the next time, until a little becomes a lot, and then consumes the person. In chasing after the pleasure itself, instead of resting in hope for that to which pleasure itself points—the fullness of God's kingdom—these misguided people create an idol and destroy themselves. They worship and serve the creation rather than the Creator (Rom. 1:25).

Denial of Reality

The act of denial takes a prominent place in the drunk's theology. His god is wine. His god is a ridiculous counterfeit idol. It is ridiculous and impotent to save him. It will only destroy him, slowly. Yet this god possesses him. To own up to its sovereignty over his life would mean confessing that he had hit rock bottom—socially, spiritually, and humanly speaking (cognitive dissonance). It is a confession of complete bankruptcy.

Instead of facing the problem, the drunk rationalizes his behavior. All idolaters do this: their god is stupid, but they worship it anyway and then make excuses for doing so. Isaiah wrote about this:

> The carpenter stretches a line; he marks it out with a pencil. He shapes it with planes and marks it with a compass. He shapes it into the figure of a man, with the beauty of a man, to dwell in a house. He cuts down cedars, or he chooses a cypress tree or an oak and lets it grow strong among the trees of the forest. He plants a cedar and the rain nourishes it. Then it becomes fuel for a man. He takes a part of it and warms himself; he kindles a fire and bakes bread. Also he makes a god and worships it; he makes it an idol and falls down before it. Half of it he burns in the fire. Over the half he eats meat; he roasts it and is satisfied. Also he warms himself and says, "Aha, I am warm, I have seen the fire!" And the rest of it he makes into a god, his idol, and falls down to it and worships it. He prays to it and says, "Deliver me, for you are my god!" (Is. 44:13–17).

After all that *human* input, the fool falls down and worships the very thing he made as if it could deliver him—when *he* is *its* creator!

The drunk does the same thing. Well, of course, he doesn't literally fall down and worship booze; but he does succumb to drunkenness over and over for the false deliverance it provides—deliverance from the cares of this life.

So the drunkard ends up denying God's reality in two ways: 1) he denies that he himself has a problem, and 2) he runs from God's reality by seeking the false one drunkenness provides.

A great portrayal of the drunk and his follies appears in the play "John Bull's Other Island" by George Bernard Shaw. Shaw was an atheist, socialist, and profligate, so we can expect him to write with some authority on human vice. Whatever the case, his drunkard has several insightful qualities.

Shaw created the character Tim Haffigan, whom he describes thusly: "Haffigan is a stunted, shortnecked, smallheaded, redhaired man of about 30, with reddened nose and furtive eyes. He is dressed in seedy black, almost clerically, and might be a tenth-rate schoolmaster ruined by drink." Despite his lack of elegance, the Irishman Haffigan is not lacking in the drunk's version of denial, and yet savvy. Talking with the main character, Broadbent, the discussion goes:

BROADBENT. Try a whisky and soda.

TIM [sobered]. There you touch the national weakness, sir.
[Piously] Not that I share it myself. I've seen too much of the mischief of it.

BROADBENT [pouring the whisky]. Say when.

TIM. Not too strong. [Broadbent stops and looks enquiringly at him]. Say half-an-half. [Broadbent, somewhat startled by this demand, pours a little more, and again stops and looks]. Just a drain more: the lower half o the tumbler doesn't hold a fair half. Thank ya.

BROADBENT [laughing]. You Irishmen certainly do know how to drink. [Pouring some whisky for himself] Now that's my poor English idea of a whisky and soda.

TIM. And a very good idea it is too. Drink is the curse o me unhappy country. I take it myself because I've a weak heart and a poor digestion; but in principle I'm a teetotaler.[1]

Now, I don't know if Tim's particular gifts and vices are obvious here, so I will elaborate. First, the vices—the first of which is denial. Haffigan begins saying he does not touch the stuff. He is a teetotaler. And yet, he gives in and takes a glass. Then, we find out he has quite an experienced eye for filling up a tumbler to an actual half! Well, he must have had considerable experience to learn *that*. And with the eagerness he displayed in demanding it, we can surmise he really did enjoy the stuff after all. Then, once he has acquiesced against his claim to be a teetotaler, he makes excuses for his behavior: he only does it for health reasons, but in *principle* he abstains.

The truth, for the drunk, however, is that he was subservient to his idol the whole time. This is why the traditional 12-step program of Alcoholics Anonymous starts with number one: "We admitted we were powerless over alcohol—that our lives had become unmanageable."

This is a confession of reality.

Forbidding alcohol has no better effect on one's perception of reality. The American cynic, Ambrose Bierce, was correct when he defined rum as "fiery liquors that

---

1. I have modernized and Americanized Shaw's portrayal of the native Irishman's English.

produce madness in total abstainers."[2] More Christians have been consigned to hell by other Christians for the alleged sin of drinking alcohol than probably all other sins combined—and yet this is terribly misguided to say the least. Prohibition is its own type of denial of reality. Instead of escaping through substance abuse, these deniers escape through twisted religious beliefs, adding to God's Word, drawing lines God did not—and thus, creating a false world of "godliness" with which God has nothing to do.

Oftentimes, in fact, this mentality is part of a broader misguided view of "the world." This view thinks that things of "this world" are evil and should thus be avoided. This includes all things like dancing, "secular" music, alcohol, tobacco, movies (most other forms of art), and many other things. These are opposed to being "heavenly minded" with things like prayer, going to church, paying tithes, waiting for "the rapture," etc. And ultimately, God is coming to deliver us from this world via the ultimate form of escapism, the rapture.

It may seem, in some cases, that this aversion to "the world" is biblical. John, after all, does teach things that sound like this: "love not the world" (1 John 2:15), "the whole world lies in the power of the evil one" (5:19). But this is to misunderstand the word "world." It does not mean "planet earth" as we use it today. It means the system of things that were then in place, the way of living that was outside of God's law: the Roman Empire, the Jewish Temple, nonbelievers, etc.

---

2. Ambrose Bierce, *The Devil's Dictionary* (New York: Dover Publications, Inc., 1993 [1911]), 110.

To extend it beyond this is to adopt a Platonic, or *Gnostic*, worldview that believed mere contact with earthly matter meant defilement and impurity. While some Christians did get mixed up with this worldview, it was not biblical. It defies the fact that God created *everything* "good," and gave His judgment upon it all collectively as "very good" (Gen. 1:31). It defies that when God decided to save man, it involved taking on the very form of that earth known as human flesh (John 1:14). And it defies God's promise of not only heaven, but a *new earth* wherein dwells righteousness (Is. 65:17; 66:22; 2 Pet. 3:13; Rev. 21:1).

The revolt against "worldliness" in the old fundamentalist sense partakes of this "touch not" worldview. It has little to do with the Bible, and more to do with a Gnostic denial of the goodness of creation and redemption. This view thinks that by abstaining from certain actions or behaviors—especially those that pertain to bodily enjoyment—we are therefore somehow "pure." There are, to be sure, lines to be drawn between godly pleasure and obvious sins, but when these lines are drawn beyond what the Bible warrants, you have entered the territory of the Pharisees, legalism, works-righteousness, etc. And to the extent this confounds the works-righteousness with "being spotless from the world," it has partaken of Gnosticism. And this is a pure denial of God's created reality, no better than the drunk's own substance-based escapism.

Besides, the prohibitionist denial of certain things is rarely ever consistent. Charles Spurgeon, the great Baptist preacher, once told a story along these lines:

You have heard, perhaps, of the very pious man, who entered a monastery in order that he might spend all his time in devotion; so, when the time came for the brethren to go into the fields to work, he did not leave his cell; he was too spiritual to handle a hoe or a spade, so he continued in communion with angels. He was very much surprised, however, when the time came for the brotherhood to assemble in the refectory, that he was not called; and after waiting till the demands of hunger overcame the claims of his spiritual being, he went to the prior, and asked why he had not been called to the meal, and he was informed that, as he was so spiritual that he could not work, it was thought that he was probably so spiritual that he could not eat; and, at any rate, the laws of the monastery did not permit him to eat until he had earned what he needed. ("Thought Condemned, yet Commanded" *MTP*, Vol 52, p. 82)

Consistency in defining "worldliness" means that not all things in the world are "worldly" in the evil sense. Not all things in earth are "worldly." While some things can be abused, they need not therefore be refused. As noted earlier, it makes no more sense to ban alcohol that it does to ban other things that people abuse—be it sex or food. Yet most prohibitionists allow that food and sex can be used for bodily enjoyment despite their addictive nature and potential for abuse. They have just thereby undermined their own case against alcohol.

Chapter 9

CHEESE FOR
THAT WHINE

As we saw earlier (Chapter 4), God sometimes speaks of drunkenness as a symbol of His judgment on society (Ezek. 23:28–34; Lam. 4:21–22). It is important to remember that this prophecy was given against God's rebellious people. This becomes all the more important today when we recognize that when Christians rebel against God's standards—for example, by absolutely *forbidding* the enjoyment of wine and alcohol—then they should expect God to be displeased with them. In another twist of irony, then, we ought to expect the Christian beer police and wine Nazis to be the ones who end up staggering to and fro under God's judgment.

If we consider this judgment intellectually speaking, this is exactly what we see: dizzy interpretations of Scripture, blurred visions of God's will, and stuttering, stammering, staggeringly misguided arguments. Like a drunk trying to convince the police he's OK to drive, these fearful and indignant Christians try to convince us that their contortions of Scripture can walk a straight line. But the sobriety test does not lie. Neither does sound exegesis of the Bible.

"Total Apostasy"

Examples of modern preachers acting this way are not hard to find. I have chosen two fairly well-known pro-hibitionists at random—Jack Van Impe (the so-called "Walking Bible"), and creation evangelist Kent Hovind. These men make their case very clearly and their arguments represent the position of many other preachers.

We'll start with Jack Van Impe. He has been a leading fundamentalist televangelist and Bible prophecy teacher for sixty years. He has reached literally millions of people with his views. He stands as an example of those who believe the Bible teaches total abstinence from alcohol.

In a recent interview with charismatic power-evangelist Rod Parsely, Van Impe summarized his view. He gave a brief diatribe on alcohol as an example of the state of the church today in "total apostasy."[1]

Total apostasy? Are you serious?

In order to maintain his firm condemnation of "liquor" he quoted the favorite passage, Proverbs 23:31. (I have a theory that this verse has been abused more than alcohol itself has been abused. The fundamentalist world really could profit from a Proverbs 23:31 Anonymous program.) "Look not upon the wine when it's red, when it shows its colour . . . when it moves itself—fermentation." We have seen already how this abuse of Scripture is untenable. But Van Impe—who is well-known for having so many passages of Scripture memorized—pretends he

---

1. All quotations of Van Impe come from this clip: http://www.youtube.com/watch?v=fLDCb9hzt2E (accessed Jan. 31, 2011).

is also a linguistic scholar: "I've got every word classified from Genesis to Revelation on the subject of wine: you're never allowed to drink wine once it ferments."

Of course, he is assuming the very thing he is trying to prove. This is circular reasoning. First, he assumes that the Bible forbids drinking fermented wine (misinterpreting Proverbs 23), then he assumes that any positive mention of wine in Scripture must therefore refer to non-fermented wine. But is he right about either of these assumptions?

He expounds: "The Bible said that *yayin* and *oinos*—the Greek words—meant 'grape juice.' You can drink all the grape juice you can hold, but when it ferments, No!, because no drunkard can enter heaven (1 Cor. 6:10, Gal. 5:19–21). . . . Apostasy!" Van Impe's position is clear: not only is drinking a sin, it is apostasy (departing from the faith). In other words, a glass of wine will send you to hell. He brackets his comments with the denunciation: "Total apostasy. . . . Apostasy!"

Unfortunately, what falls in the middle of those brackets hardly backs up his bluster (which is why most people bluster to begin with, isn't it?). *First*, Van Impe has some linguistic confusion. He calls "*yayin* and *oinos*" "Greek words," when in fact, only the second word is Greek. *Yayin* is Hebrew, as you already know by now.

Second, he says that the Bible tells us these words mean "grape juice." Really? Where? There's no definition section in the Bible. Only a teetotaler preaching to a roomful of teetotalers could get away with that statement. The Bible *nowhere* stops to define exactly what is meant by the word. Instead, the context tells us what

the words best mean, and in no case is there any reason to doubt that *yayin* or *oinos* are alcoholic. As we saw
in Chapter 2, the first mention of wine requires that it
be alcoholic, and this continues throughout. We have
seen that there are in fact *other* words that mean "grape
juice," and God could easily have chosen those words if
He wanted to convey that meaning. He rarely ever did.
We will see this type of linguistic issue again in a minute.

Third, Van Impe contradicts himself in the very next
sentence: he says that we are never allowed to drink *yayin* or *oinos* "when it ferments." This means that they are
no longer mere grape juice "when it ferments." In other
words, the Bible says that *yayin* and *oinos* mean grape
juice, except when it means they are not (which . . . cough
. . . ahem . . . is the vast majority of the time). Van Impe
needs to deal with this obvious problem in his view.

Fourth, Van Impe swindles his audience: his argument assumes that anyone imbibing fermented wine is
automatically a "drunkard" and cannot enter the kingdom of heaven. But Scripture does not present things this
way. A biblical drunkard is a habitual drunkard. This person drinks, passes out, and says, "When shall I awake? I
must have another drink" (Prov. 23:35). The King James
renders this verse: "I will seek it yet again." This means
the drunkard *repeats* his folly day-in-day-out. He is totally given to wine and numb to the world; he is not someone
who simply enjoys fermented drink responsibly or only
occasionally. Van Impe has created a classic fallacy called
a "false dichotomy"—a false division or a false choice. The
avoidance of drunkenness is not about the choice: either
drink or totally abstain, but rather about personal re-

sponsibility in *how much* you choose to drink.

While biblical morality is clearly objective, and most things are black-and-white (a lie is a lie, is it not? Adultery is adultery), some things simply are not. By the standard of Van Impe's false choice, a single drink makes you a drunkard. By the same standard, one moment in a comfortable chair makes you a sluggard, one bite a glutton, one short-cut a cheater, one paraphrase a liar, one desire a fornicator, one spanking a child abuser, etc., etc. This is simply not the way God designed so much of Christian life and human conscience.

Fifth, and by the way, it is also worth noting that it is not the case that "you can drink all the grape juice you can hold." As we saw earlier, gluttony is just as damnable a sin as drunkenness. So gorging oneself on grape juice (who would want to?) would be both sinful and dangerous.

So Van Impe's claims and arguments do not line up with Scripture, and thus his teaching on alcohol should not be taken seriously despite the sternness of his denunciations of apostasy (perhaps we should say especially *because* of his vociferous condemnations). On the contrary, *he* is the one in serious error—the error of robbing Christians of faith, joy, love, and maturity. The issue is not "total apostasy," as he says, but rather his own teetotal apostasy. It is a message of fear and childishness in which Christians are forbidden joy, freedom, and the opportunity to grow in grace and self-control.

Hovind's Hiccups

Similar to Van Impe's arguments, Kent Hovind, a normally brilliant creation scientist, also makes a terribly ignorant and deceptive argument concerning alcohol. He teaches very similar factual errors about the word for "wine" in the Greek language. First, he argues that the Greek language contains only one word for "wine." He goes on to say that this lone word—"*oinos*"—can mean many things: "grape juice, grape jelly, grape syrup, alcoholic wine. . . . If it comes from the grape, it's called 'wine.'"[2] When it says "wine," he then argues, it does not mean "fermented."

Unfortunately, this is not accurate. There is another Greek word for wine: it is "*gleukos*." We get our word "glucose" (plant or fruit sugar) from this. It literally means "sweet juice," and refers to "new wine" or freshly pressed grape juice.

So already, despite Hovind's insistence otherwise, there is a clear distinction made in the Greek language: *oinos* means "wine," and *gleukos* means "grape juice." So if the New Testament writers ever wanted to insist on grape juice the way modern fundamentalists do, they could easily have done so by using the word *gleukos*. Now let us review all of the instances in which they could have done so.

While the normal word *oinos* appears in the New Testament 33 times, this word for "new wine" or "grape juice," *gleukos*, appears a whopping once. But it gets even more interesting than this.

Even freshly pressed grape juice was stored for a period of time; even "fresh" juice was fermented a little in this time period before it was bottled for later consump-

2.   All quotations of Hovind come from the clip: http://www. youtube.com/watch?v=fLDCb9hzt2E, (accessed Jan. 31, 2011).

tion. This was a commonly known fact, and one could even get drunk on this "fresh" stuff if they drank enough. Thus, even the lone reference to "grape juice" in the New Testament (Acts 2:13) is used in the context of alleged drunkenness. On the day of Pentecost, after the apostles received the Holy Spirit and began speaking in other tongues, all the bystanders were amazed. "But others mocking said, 'They are filled with new wine [*gleukos*]'" (Acts 2:13).

The phrase "filled with" is a reference to excess. And this is exactly what Peter understands them to say. Thus he refutes the allegation of drunkenness: he says, "these people are not drunk, as you suppose, since it is only the third hour of the day" (Acts 2:15). It was only nine in the morning! There was hardly time in the day so far to get drunk, and who gets drunk that early anyway?

Of course, the point here is that even the mildest form of "wine" in that culture was known to be alcoholic enough that one could drink to excess. This aside, *gleukos* still refers literally only to the more freshly bottled juice, as opposed to *oinos*. If, therefore, Scripture indeed forbids consumption of alcohol, we would expect to see *gleukos* used a lot more than just once out of 33 instances. (Doing the math, the New Testament is 97 percent in favor of the alcoholic stuff.)

Jesus: "No One Prefers New Wine"

There is only other usage of the phrase "new wine" in New Testament Greek, and that is in Matthew 9:17 (see also Mark 2:22; Luke 5:37–39). There Jesus taught about how difficult it is for people set in old ways of thinking to receive new teaching. He gave this parable: "Neither is new wine put into old wineskins. If it is, the skins burst and the wine is spilled and the skins are destroyed. But new wine is put into fresh wineskins, and so both are preserved." Here the phrase "new wine" is not *gleukos*, but two words in Greek, *oinon neon*. This literally says "new wine." And it obviously refers to wine that has not yet fermented.

Notice in this passage that the word "wine" (*oinos*) itself was not sufficient for Jesus to make His point about non-fermented wine. He had to qualify it: *new* wine—the kind that is fresh-pressed and not yet fermented. And yet this new wine is specifically expected to become fermented: that is why the bottles (skins) are expected to expand. If old, already-stretched-out wineskins are subjected again to the expansion of the fermentation process, they will simply not hold out—they will burst. So, Jesus says, "new wine is put into fresh wineskins, and so both are preserved."

So, new wine is fresh, awaiting fermentation, and old wine has completed the process of fermentation (the wineskins having expanded).

With this in mind, it is interesting that in Luke's version of the same parable, Jesus adds the following statement: "And no one after drinking old wine desires new, for he says, 'The old is good'" (Luke 5:39). Could it really be that Jesus advocated what everyone else knew, and which they all took for granted—that old, fermented wine is "good"?

And there is theology in this as well: this "good" that we taste in old wine is the same Greek word used to say "taste and see that the Lord is *good*" (Ps. 33:9; see 1 Pet. 2:3). This very goodness of God leads us to repentance (Rom. 2:4), and is itself a fruit of the Spirit we should manifest (Gal. 5:22). In other words, it does not just *taste* good, it *is* good.

Hovind then goes on to apply his wrong teaching about the lone Greek word to the Old Testament as well. Problem: the Old Testament was written in Hebrew, not Greek. And Hebrew, as we saw in Chapter 2, contains *several* words that can be translated as "wine." Nevertheless, after his incomplete Greek lesson, he proceeds to the same verse as Van Impe: Proverbs 23:31. He quotes from the King James: "Look not thou upon the wine when it is red, when it giveth his colour in the cup, *when* it moveth itself aright." Just like Van Impe, Hovind argues that this redness and color and moving refers to fermentation. Therefore, we are not to drink wine when it is fermented.

As we saw earlier, this proverb does not refer to the fermentation process, but is simply poetry describing wine's alluring appearance to the lustful and the drunkard. This seductive appearance is contrasted with the true nature of drunkenness (Prov. 23:32–35).

So all in all, Hovind has engaged in the same errors as Van Impe: he obviously has a very shallow knowledge of the original biblical languages and therefore has committed very elementary-level errors in dealing with them.

The Wedding Crasher

So far, Hovind has both misrepresented biblical Greek and wrongly imposed his misrepresentation of Greek onto the Hebrew Old Testament. With this lin-

guistic swindle in place, he then tackles the account of
Jesus turning water into wine (John 2). He addresses
that common old argument that "Jesus drank wine," to
which the scientist responds, "No, He didn't." According
to Hovind, Jesus created "grape juice, and they drank it
the same day."

For his ultimate proof here, Hovind argues: "Jesus
could not have drank alcoholic wine because it would
have gone against what the Scripture says [he points
to Proverbs 23:31 on an overhead projector]; and Jesus
didn't violate any Scriptures." The argument is abys-
mal. Assuming what he has yet to prove—that Proverbs
23:31 indeed refers to fermentation and indicates that we
should not look upon fermented grape juice—Hovind
then proceeds to assume that the wine of John 2 was unfermented, because Jesus would not have violated Proverbs 23:31's ban on fermentation.

This is dubious on more than one count. First, it is unnecessary to absolve Jesus from drinking fermented wine
in this case, because the account in John 2:1–12 never
says that Jesus drank the wine which He created (as we
saw earlier). It could well be that Jesus created fermented
wine, but drank none of it. Of course, I don't believe that
to be the case, but its possibility does render any reac-
tionary defense of Jesus unnecessary. We discussed what
Proverbs 23:31 means already, and this exposes Hovind's
interpretation as strained, forced, and unskilled.

Also, the reaction of the wedding host in John 2
makes it clear that Jesus created the kind of wine people
call "good"—old wine: "the master of the feast called the
bridegroom and said to him, 'Everyone serves the good

wine first, and when people have drunk freely, then the poor wine. But you have kept the good wine until now'" (John 2:9–10).

Yes, normally wedding planners are cheap (hard to believe considering how much they charge): serving good wine (and presumably expensive) for a brief time until people get to feeling good; then they switch to the cheap stuff hoping people are too tipsy to notice (they usually aren't). Notice the necessary role of the alcohol in this story. The "good" wine has an effect on the drinkers: they get sated, relaxed. Well, this is the type of wine Jesus created for the latter part of the party—the kind of wine that relaxes and makes people enjoy themselves. This is the good stuff—well-aged, select, expertly-made, stored, and saved for that special occasion. While Jesus could easily have made *gleukos* or "new wine," He chose to make good wine. And according to John, this was Jesus' "beginning of miracles" (2:11).

In other words, even if Jesus never drank any of the wine that wedding day, it's clear He wanted everyone else to enjoy themselves with it. Enough so, that before He fed the 5,000, healed the lame or blind, walked on water, or calmed the raging storm, He created "good" wine—old wine, fine alcoholic wine—for the wedding at Cana. The world's introduction to Jesus' miraculous power was His livening the party with about 160 gallons of the finest wine they'd ever tasted.

The Bible Butcher

But Hovind is not done. He cites Habakkuk 2:15 as a warning as well: "Woe unto him that giveth his neighbour drink." Given all that he's loaded on us so far, Hovind now expects us to believe that this passage means "There's a curse on those who supply alcohol to other people." This curse falls on "those who drive the beer truck . . . the stewardess on an airplane . . . and those that even serve it to other people."

While the verse as quoted here may seem to back his point, there is something very important Hovind leaves out: again, it's the context. Not only did he ignore the full context, he didn't even quote the whole verse. Here's what the whole passage says: "Woe to him who makes his neighbors drink—you pour out your wrath and make them drunk, *in order to gaze at their nakedness!*"

So we see here that the sin was not in the mere act of giving someone else wine. Rather, it was in the use of alcohol like a date-rape drug. It was the purposeful causing of someone to get drunk *for the express purpose of exploiting them sexually.*

The whole context of Habakkuk 2 is about a rebellious society consumed with exploitation—financially, politically, in murder, bloodshed, warfare, idolatry, and here in verse 15, in drunkenness and voyeurism. This passage does not condemn the enjoyment of alcohol as a blessing from God any more than it does the enjoyment of sex as a blessing from God. It is about exploitation and abuse, not righteous use.

Tearing Bible verses from their context is bad enough, but Hovind even makes up Bible teachings out of thin air. He says, "The Bible is very clear on the subject: 'Don't touch alcohol.'" As we have seen quite clearly so far, the Bible never forbids drinking wine; much less does it go so far as to forbid even *touching* it. The Bible says nothing of the sort, let alone does it say it "clearly" as Hovind alleges.

Furthermore, Hovind is displaying the Proverbs 23 verse as he makes this statement: "Look not thou. . . ." Were he consistent with his oversimplified, literalistic interpretation of a verse that doesn't exist—"Don't touch alcohol"—he should really do what Scripture *actually* says and forbid even *looking* at alcohol! "A Bud Light truck! Avert your eyes!"

In a mere four minutes of teaching, Hovind has managed to botch biblical Greek, impose his Greek errors onto the Hebrew Old Testament where they don't apply anyway, build assumptions on top of assumptions, ignore the context of three passages, quote only sections of passages, and make up Scripture passages to suit him. I suspect there are more fallacies lurking in there, but this should suffice to make the point: in order to maintain this strict prohibitionist view, one must be willing to ignore, pervert, contort, and lie about a lot of Scripture, as well as set aside common sense.

Part 4:
⟩ *The Finish* ⟨

Chapter 10

BEER AND DOMINION

Some audacious historians dare to trace the rise of civilization itself to the discovery of beer. In their humanistic view, men quit being hunter-gatherers as soon as they by happenstance learned that grain would ferment. This pleasant surprise gave them the motivation to find more grain. Since grain grew only sparsely in the wild, this provided an incentive to start cultivating fields. This led to organized agriculture. Abundant grain provided a need for storage, large-scale breweries, etc. Cities evolved, civilizations were built.

This is most certainly untrue. Man and man's civilization did not evolve by happenstance. God created man upright with a command to order and civilize the whole world. According to the Bible, the first sons of Adam were already productive farmers of both crops and animals. This does not, of course, diminish the role of beer and wine in society: nay, rather, it simply places it in proper perspective, as we shall see. Instead of being a happy accident that drove beast-like appetites to scramble for more buzz, beer and wine become purposeful ornaments upon a society already well-developed. They add a pleasure and a joy to adorn daily toils at their end.

The Dominion Mandate

In the beginning God created the heavens and the earth. In that process He created man and woman in His image. Then, He gave rule over the whole earth to that man and woman:

> Let them have dominion over the fish of the sea and over the birds of the heavens and over the livestock and over all the earth and over every creeping thing that creeps on the earth. . . . And God blessed them. And God said to them, "Be fruitful and multiply and fill the earth and subdue it and have dominion over the fish of the sea and over the birds of the heavens and over every living thing that moves on the earth" (Gen. 1:26–28).

This is God's original "dominion mandate" given to man. It includes power and authority over all the earth, and over all its flora and fauna. And it includes God's command that man reproduce abundantly (creating in his own image, just as God did), fill the whole earth, and "subdue it"—which means, bring it into subjection to godliness.

From your own experience, you've probably noticed that human history has been a combination of failure and success in this endeavor. Let us dwell on the successes.

In the first chapter, we saw Noah engaging in agriculture. He planted the first vineyard mentioned in the Bible. Now agriculture had already been invented hundreds of years earlier: remember, Cain was a farmer, and Abel was a shepherd. These developments and skills were passed down, especially during this time when men lived very long lives. Adam died at 930 (Gen. 5:5), and died only a few decades before Noah—the ninth generation from Adam—was born. Adam's son Seth died only a few years before Noah was born. Adam's grandson Enos saw Noah born, and Noah was his great-great-great-great-great grandson. What all this means, of course, is that Noah would have learned agricultural techniques that had been honed and perfected over the course of about one thousand years. So he was no beginner when he landed afresh upon the mountains of Ararat. It is very possible, therefore, that his was not the first vineyard ever planted, nor the first wine ever pressed, fermented, and enjoyed.

In short, man was born for dominion in this earth, and this entails organized planning, development, implementation, work, and progress. And the fruit of the vine has been the "end of the day" refreshment and enjoyment since the days of Noah, but really, probably since early in Adam's life.

And not only did God ordain man for dominion and create him in His image a creative being, but God Himself established a cycle of work and rest for man to follow—both daily and weekly. During the creation week, God did a little of His design every day for six days (Gen 1:2–31). Each day He worked some, and then rested to evaluate His work. He began again the next day. Then after six days, when God had seen His work through its completion, He rested for a full day—the seventh day. Completing his work-rest cycle, God blessed the day of rest especially:

> Thus the heavens and the earth were finished, and all the host of them. And on the seventh day God finished his work that he had done, and he rested on

the seventh day from all his work that he had done.
So God blessed the seventh day and made it holy, because on it God rested from all his work that he had
done in creation (Gen. 2:1–3).

As His image, we follow this same cycle of daily work
and rest, and of weekly work and rest. We constantly work
to glorify God and to spread His dominion on earth, and
we constantly rest in turn that we may assess our progress and refresh ourselves for the next day. In doing so, it
is good to have reminder of the joy set before us.

Hope and Refreshment

Work and labor are often monotonous—whether white
or blue collar. Things can progress downward: tedious,
boring, old, difficult, stressful, unbearable, nervous
breakdown. Men lose their drive and ambition. Without
some promise or hope for something better in the future,
all hope is quickly and easily lost.

It is good to have both long-term and short-term
goals at which to aim. This helps keep a vision—a promise of what the future will be—in front of all involved.
And it is good to have regular reminders of the goodness
of that future. These should be simple, small, and joyful
encouragements of every possible form.

The role of wine as a foretaste of the fullness of the
kingdom plays a beneficial (lawful *and* helpful) role here.
Nothing refreshes at the end of the day like a cold beer.
Nothing resurrects the joy of a work-weary heart like
blood of the grape, that spark of enjoyment reigniting the
fire of hope and progress for the evening and the next

day. Wine and beer do not have significance only for religious or periodically festive occasions. They are also part of the daily liturgy of work and calling—of waking, planning, toiling, progressing, assessing, *resting*. It is that renewed foretaste of the fullness of the kingdom that helps keep our hearts, minds, and bodies joyful and hopeful toward that prize.

One of the best businesses ever to capture this ideal for a workplace was the beer company founded by Arthur Guinness in 1759. He had such a strong long-term vision that he signed the original lease for his factory's property for *nine thousand years*.[1] He was a godly man, founding the first Sunday schools in Ireland,[2] and yet his view of Christianity was much more substantial than most today. It involved more than church on Sunday and stories for children; it was a vision that involved the image of God and dominion on earth, planning, work, progress, charity, and hopeful rest. Like Adam and Eve, Arthur Guinness knew that most of a person's service to God takes place during the other six days of the week. A wonderful recent book on the impact of the Guinness company captures this sentiment. In his study of the company, the author Stephen Mansfield learned a valuable lesson:

> We are used to religion that is sometimes an escape from daily life and faith as fixation on life in another world. What Arthur Guinness founded

1. Stephen Mansfield, *The Search for God and Guinness: A Biography of the Beer that Changed the World* (Nashville, TN: Thomas nelson, 2009), xxvii.
2. Mansfield, xxvii.

was a venture propelled by faith, yes—but by a kind of faith that inspires men to make their work in this world an offering to God, to understand craft and discipline, love of labor and skills transferred from father to son as sacred things. It was a venture of faith that took the fruit of the earth and, through study and strain, made of it something of greater value. Indeed, much of the great 250-year history of Guinness beer is a story in which wealth is gained through faith-inspired excellence and then used to serve others for the glory of God.[3]

And Mr. Guinness left quite a legacy. At times in the company's history, it was company policy that workers be allotted daily pints of the beer. In addition to many other fringe benefits, as we will see momentarily, this is just the type of daily refreshment that recharges the vision and motivates the soul to strive again the next day. Mr. Mansfield, a Christian himself, learned this also. His shallow view of beer was changed by his study:

And I confess, as an outsider to drinking and beer, I used to think it was all about the buzz, that drinking anything with alcohol was about escaping and drifting into a sloshy other world. But now I know something I did not before. Beer is not simply a means of drunkenness nor is it merely a lubricant to grease the skids of sin. Beer, well respected and rightly consumed, can be a gift of God. It is one of his mysteries, which it was

---

3. Mansfield, xvi.

his delight to conceal and the glory of kings to search out. And men enjoy it to mark their days and celebrate their moments with their brothers in the face of what life brings.[4]

I would change only one part of this wonderful revelation: the words "can be." When "well respected and rightly consumed," there is no "can be" about it. Beer *IS* a gift from God.

Just as Jesus said, "No one after drinking old wine desires new, for he says, 'The old is good,'" we can easily see how a thirst for that "good" gives men and women that little incentive they need to keep going the next day. We can easily imagine the Guinness factory worker ending his day with his allotted two pints: cold, refreshing, smooth. "Ahhh." And he says, "This is *good*." And to be involved in producing that good for millions of others so they can end their day with the hope and rest expressed by "Ahhh" is to be involved in a much larger good.

Charity and Dominion

Most people think of charity as giving money on occasion to organizations that do specific good works for the poor, needy, etc. This much is true. Unfortunately, this is all most people think of it. But Christian charity is much broader than that.

One of the ways the Guinness company spread God's kingdom-charity is through the care it showed for its workers. It has historically paid its workers much higher wages than average (thereby recruiting and retaining the

---

4. Mansfield, xxv–xxvi.

best and brightest talent, while helping others who might otherwise have been left poor). But this was not all. Mansfield relates the following Guinness company benefits from a 1928 company report (at the height of international corporate greed right before the Great Depression):

- All employees with their wives and children enjoyed the services of an on-site clinic staffed by full-time doctors night and day; these doctors also made house calls.

- Medical services included company-dedicated dentists, pharmacists, nurses, home sanitation consultants, and a masseuse.

- Retirees received pensions, in some cases even when they never contributed to the fund. Pensions extended to widows.

- Most funeral expenses for company families and family members were paid by the company.

- The company had its own bank, and provided mortgages for company families.

- The company spurred living standards with domestic skill competitions. It gave cash awards for sewing, cooking, decorating, gardening, and hat making. The same was true for crafts, trades, and sports of all kinds.

- The company provided concerts and lectures for moral and intellectual improvement, especially for housewives.

- Guinness paid for employees' education: they could advance in technical school, trades, side-businesses, or more advanced education. The company paid all and provided a library and lounges for study.

- The company provided paid vacations including train fares and spending cash.[5]

Many of the workers enjoying these benefits had just fought a decade earlier in World War I, but they did not fear losing their benefits: Guinness guaranteed their jobs would be available for them when they returned.[6]

Yet these workers were entitled to none of these things. No business owes anything to its workers except a fair-market compensation (and thus whatever the parties agree upon, Luke 20:1–16). All of these special benefits were *subsidies—Christian charity distributed through regular business.*

What Guinness has done is use its enormous wealth to spread God's kingdom, improve society, improve people's lives on a very broad scale, and in a way that motivates and empowers the people themselves to work hard, do good, improve themselves and others, and to be charitable. It all stems from one of the Guinness family member's own belief: "You cannot make money from people unless you are willing for people to make money from you."[7]

---

5. Mansfield, xix–xxii.
6. Mansfield, xxviii.
7. Mansfield, xxx.

This is the essence of charity: spreading a foretaste of goodness that motivates and inspires the once-needy to improve themselves and then themselves do good for others. And it is probably not a stretch to say that the Guinness company has done this more often and better than most of the churches that have existed during their 250-year existence.

Beer and Freedom

Notice that Guinness created this kingdom of industry, productivity, blessing, and charity without the need of a single government law mandating health insurance, welfare, wage controls, etc. They simply took a Christian vision coupled with Christian ethics and created the best working environment around—*voluntarily*.

This is the essence of Christian freedom: it draws from God's dominion mandate, loves God and man, and serves both. It finds a way to address both man's needs and joys, create capital, give and therefore meet more of those needs, and the cycle repeats.

Mr. Guinness had been influenced by the great revivalist John Wesley. As part of preaching the gospel, Wesley emphasized the proper use of money. One of his sermons on the topic has left us this now famous mantra concerning money: "make all you can, save all you can, give all you can." Mr. Guinness put this into practice well.

And thus he spread God's kingdom and Christian ethics *freely*. He intended to promote a free Christian society by example, not depending upon rules of force to make other people pay, or a government to shoulder the burden.

This is the great error of our prohibitionist brethren. They could never achieve their unbiblical, joy-stealing purpose in a free society; and they were never content only to lead by example even if they could have. But they had little political power and no organization. The lust for power and control of society, however, made them useful tools for those who did have the power and wealth, but not the votes. Indeed, there was another such group wishing to ban alcohol—the eugenicists, who believed they could social engineer a more hard-working society if people were forced to be sober. These extraordinarily wealthy liberals and corporatists organized campaigns to grab power and impose their view through the force of law. They easily recruited the votes of Christian zealots for their cause, while the liberals themselves provided the money and the political organization. If the Christians could not persuade, therefore, they would sell out, join the unbelievers, and use the sword. And after long efforts and manipulations, they succeeded.

(Of course, when prohibition failed as a social and legal experiment, the liberals blamed the whole thing on the fundamentalist Christians and pietists.)

As we know, the result was disastrous to the economy. What was once fairly free became a black market which favored gang activity and government corruption. The mafya got rich (and more widespread and influential), the progressive liberals got more government power, and freedom died.

Nevertheless, the prohibitionists—the mixture of liberal progressives and fundamentalist Christians—blamed all the social evils on the desire for alcohol rather than their intrusion into people's lives and the imposition of government force. One famous evangelist, now infamous, even blamed the many tragedies of the Kennedy family upon the fact that they positioned themselves to sell alcohol when prohibition was lifted.[8] Of course, if Christian tyrants had never helped force through prohibition to begin with, Joseph Kennedy would never have had that opportunity, would he? If anyone's to blame, I suspect the prohibitionists should get a share in it.

As is almost universally true, when you change one thing by government force, you create a series of worse problems down the line. Economists and political scientists call this the "law of unintended consequences." And boy did prohibition cause its share.

After the dry law was lifted, compromises were made in order to ensure a number of political promises that, like all political promises, had little chance of ever helping anyone except the tiny few. In short, many of the laws left in place to regulate the system have created such a lopsided advantage for the largest few beer companies that Americans were left with low-quality beer and little choice of much else. A so-called "three-tier system" places distribution in control of the major brewers, leaving smaller brewers (of almost always better quality and variety of product) at the mercy of these big guys who just happen to be their major competitors. Bigger brewers can control all product display in local stores, and thus monopolize the space for their own products. It's still, I say, a government-imposed tyranny over alcohol, and

---

8. See Jimmy Swaggart, *Alcohol: America's Greatest Problem* (Baton Rouge, LA: Jimmy Swaggart Ministries, 1984), 27–30.

it's a vestige of ignorant, fearful, envious Christians imposing their twisted view by government force. The "big three," as they call them, control distribution and marketing arrangements, and thus are able to crowd out the little guys who are dependent upon the big guys. Why not just change the laws, you ask? Because the big three control a "beer lobby" which exerts tremendous influence on the legislators. The beer lobby contributes millions: this keeps the politicians interested in keeping the laws as they are, since they obviously keep money flowing back to the politicians.

On top of this, wine, beer, and spirits are taxed heavily in proportion to other items, making these healthful and joyful products more expensive for average families. Christians readily join in public calls for more taxes on alcohol (or tobacco), calling them "sin taxes"—taxes on things they consider vices to begin with. By this they hope to raise more money for the State (for what purpose?) while simultaneously placing a disincentive to the alleged "sin" of the product. Of course, it is really not sin to consume and use these products; the label "sin" simply makes an easy tool for imposing one's biases on society while economically punishing others who disagree. We could even call such unjust and selective taxation "theft." Theft or not, the real sin lies not in the use of alcohol, but in the use of government coercion to enforce one's superstitions about alcohol.

In other words, misguided Christian zealotry has helped bring about nothing but diminished quality, perpetual tyranny, political corruption, and tremendous cost to many innocent people. In fact, prohibition resulted in nothing but large beer companies being in control of the very laws Christians wanted to control in the first place. Is this the ideal of Christian dominion and charity in society? No, it is God's judgment on a society in which Christians partner with tyrants. Give me God, Guinness, and my freedom any day. Every day.

Conclusion

The lesson of this book is one of blessing, joy, and maturity. This chapter has been about maturity—godly work and dominion—regularly punctuated by drops of blessing reminding us of the fullness of the kingdom that yet remains in the future. This book repudiates and ridicules the fearful and unbiblical agenda of the prohibitionists and forbidders in order to return to the biblical teaching of joy and hope—a joy and hope that exist now as foretastes upon which we may return daily to our callings of work, toil, community, and progress.

If you take from this book an attitude merely of license to indulge in feasting and drinking, then you have not learned the book's lesson. Worse, you will be doomed to run into the opposite life of slack, ease, and perhaps even drunkenness, depression, and despair. I can only encourage you, then, to reread this chapter, if not the whole book, before you drink and rest. If you cannot come to grasp with the role of alcohol as a foretaste of joy to come, then perhaps you should abstain.

Drink without work is sloth. Work without drink is slavery. Work and then drink is society. It points to salvation. Embrace it.

Recommended Resources

Beer Wars. DVD. Directed by Anat Baron 2009. Gravitas Studio, 2009. 90 min.

Kenneth L. Gentry, Jr., *God Gave Wine: What the Bible Says About Alcohol* (Lincoln, CA: Oakdown, 2001).

James B. Jordan, "Faith and Rest," in *Primeval Saints: Studies in the Patriarchs of Genesis* (Moscow, ID: Canon Press, 2001), pp. 41–50..

Stephen Mansfield, *The Search for God and Guinness: A Biography of the Beer that Changed the World* (Nashville: Thomas Nelson, 2009).

Garrett Peck, *The Prohibition Hangover: Alcohol in America from Demon Rum to Cult Cabernet* (Rutgers University Press, 2009).

_____, "Winemaking in Ancient Israel," http://www.prohibitionhangover.com/israelwine.html (accessed February 15, 2011).

Jim West, *Drinking With Calvin and Luther: A History of Alcohol in the Church* (Lincoln, CA: Oakdown, 2003).